Edna Lyall

**We two**

Vol. III

Edna Lyall

**We two**
*Vol. III*

ISBN/EAN: 9783337040079

Printed in Europe, USA, Canada, Australia, Japan

Cover: Foto ©ninafisch / pixelio.de

More available books at **www.hansebooks.com**

# WE TWO

A NOVEL

BY

EDNA LYALL

AUTHOR OF "DONOVAN," ETC.

"Men are so made as to resent nothing more impatiently than to be treated as criminal for opinions which they deem true."—SPINOZA.

"We two are a multitude."—OVID.

IN THREE VOLUMES.
VOL. III.

LONDON:
HURST AND BLACKETT, PUBLISHERS,
13, GREAT MARLBOROUGH STREET.
1884.

*All rights reserved.*

# WE TWO.

## CHAPTER I.

### BRIAN AS AVENGER.

A paleness took the poet's cheek ;
'Must I drink here?' he seemed to seek
The lady's will with utterance meek.
'Ay, ay,' she said, 'it so must be,'
(And this time she spake cheerfully)
'Behoves thee know world's cruelty.'
E. B. BROWNING.

THE trial of Luke Raeburn, on the charge of having published a blasphemous libel in a pamphlet entitled 'Bible Miracles,' came on in the Court of Queen's Bench early in December. It excited a great deal of interest. Some people hoped that the revival of an almost obsolete law would really help to check the spread of heterodox views, and praised Mr. Pogson for his energy and religious zeal. These were chiefly well-meaning folks, not much given to the study of precedents. Some people of a more liberal turn read the pamphlet in question, and were surprised to see that matter quite as heterodox might be found in many high-class reviews which lay about on drawing-room tables, the only difference being that the articles in the reviews were written in somewhat ambiguous language by fashionable agnostics, and that 'Bible Miracles' was a plain, blunt, sixpenny tract, avowedly written for the people by the people's tribune.

This general interest and attention, once excited, gave rise to the following results : to an indiscriminate and wholesale condemnation of 'that odious Raeburn who was always seeking notoriety;' to an immense demand for 'Bible. Miracles,' which in three months reached its fiftieth thousand; and to a considerable crowd in Westminster Hall on the first day of the trial, to watch the entrance and exit of the celebrities.

Erica had been all day in the court. She had written her article for the *Daily Review* in pencil during the break for luncheon; but, as time wore on, the heated atmosphere of the place, which was crammed to suffocation, became intolerable to her. She grew whiter and whiter, began to hear the voices indistinctly, and to feel as if her arms did not belong to her. It would never do to faint in court, and vexed as she was to leave, she took the first opportunity of speaking to her father.

'I think I must go,' she whispered; 'I can't stand this heat.'

'Come now, then,' said Raeburn, 'and I can see you out. This witness has nothing worth listening to. Take notes for me, Tom. I'll be back directly.'

They had only just passed the door leading into Westminster Hall, however, when Tom sent a messenger hurrying after them. An important witness had that moment been called, and Raeburn, who was, as usual, conducting his own case, could not possibly miss the evidence.

'I can go alone,' said Erica. 'Don't stop.'

But even in his haste, Raeburn, glancing at the crowd of curious faces, was thoughtful for his child.

'No,' he said, hurriedly. 'Wait a moment, and I'll send someone to you.'

She would have been wiser if she had followed him back into the court; but, having once escaped from the intolerable atmosphere, she was not at all inclined to return to it. She waited where he had left her, just within Westminster Hall, at the top of the steps leading from the entrance to the court. The grandeur of the place, its magnificent proportions, terminating in the great, upward sweep of steps, and the mellow stained window, struck her more than ever after coming from the crowded and inconvenient little court within. The vaulted roof, with its quaintly-carved angels, was for the most part dim and shadowy, but here and there a ray of sunshine, slanting in through the clerestory windows, changed the sombre tones to a golden splendour. Erica, very susceptible to all high influences, was more conscious of the ennobling influence of light, and space, and beauty than of the curious eyes which were watching her from below. But all at once her attention was drawn to a group of men who stood near her, and her thoughts were suddenly brought back to the hard, every-day world, from which for a brief moment she had escaped. With a quick, apprehensive glance, she noted that among them was a certain Sir Algernon Wyte, a man who never lost an opportunity of insulting her father.

'Did you see the fellow?' said one of the group. 'He came to the door just now.'

'And left his fair daughter to be a spectacle to men and angels!' said Sir Algernon.

Then followed words so monstrous, so intolerable, that Erica, accustomed as she was to discourtesies, broke down altogether. It was so heartless, so cruelly false, and she was so perfectly defenceless! A wave of burning colour swept over her face. If she could but have gone away—have hidden herself from those cruel eyes! But her knees trembled so fearfully that, had she tried to move, she must have fallen. Sick and giddy, the flight of steps looked to her like a precipice. She could only lean for support against the grey-stone mouldings of the doorway, while tears, which for once she could not restrain, rushed to her eyes.

Oh! if Tom or the professor, or some one would but come to her! Such moments as those are not measured by earthly time; the misery seemed to her age-long, though it was in reality brief enough, for Brian, coming into Westminster Hall, had actually heard Sir Algernon's shameful slander, and pushing his way through the crowd, was beside her almost immediately.

The sight of his face checked her tears. It positively frightened her by its restrained yet intense passion.

'Miss Raeburn,' he said, in a clear, distinct voice, plainly heard by the group below, 'this is not a fit place for you. Let me take you home.'

He spoke much more formally than was his wont, yet in his actions he used a sort of authority, drawing her hand within his arm, leading her rapidly through the crowd, which opened before them. For that one bitter-sweet moment she belonged to him. He was her sole, and therefore her rightful, protector. A minute more, and they stood in Palace Yard. He hastily called a hansom.

In the pause she looked up at him, and would

have spoken her thanks; but something in his manner checked her. He had treated her so exactly as if she belonged to him, that to thank him seemed almost as absurd as it would have done to thank her father. Then a sudden fear made her say instead,

'Are you coming home?'

'I will come to see that you are safely back presently,' he said, in a voice unlike his own. 'But I must see that man first.'

'No, no,' she said, beginning to tremble again. 'Don't go back. Please, please don't go!'

'I must,' he said, putting her into the hansom. Then, speaking very gently—'Don't be afraid; I will be with you almost directly.'

He closed the doors, gave the address to the driver, and turned away.

Erica was conscious of a vague relief as the fresh winter wind blew upon her. She shut her eyes, that she might not see the passers-by, only longing to get away—right away, somewhere beyond the reach of staring eyes and cruel tongues. One evening years ago she remembered coming out of St. James's Hall with

Tom, and having heard a woman in Regent Street insulted in precisely the same language that had been used to her to-day. She remembered how the shrill, passionate cry had rung down the street—'How dare you insult me!' And remembered, too, how she had wondered whether perfect innocence would have been able to give that retort. She knew now that her surmise had been correct. The insult had struck her dumb for the time. Even now, as the words returned to her with a pain intolerable, her tears rained down. It seemed to her that for once she could no more help crying than she could have helped bleeding when cut.

Then once more her thoughts turned to Brian with a warmth of gratitude which in itself relieved her. He was a man worth knowing, a friend worth having. Yet how awful his face had looked as he came towards her. Only once in her whole life had she seen such a look on a man's face. She had seen it in her childhood on her father's face, when he had first heard of a shameful libel which affected those nearest and dearest to him. She had been far too young to understand the meaning of it, but she well remembered that silent, consuming wrath; she remembered running away by herself with the sort of half fearful delight of a child's new discovery—'Now I know how men look when they *kill!*'

All at once, in the light of that old recollection, the truth flashed upon her. She smiled through her tears, a soft glow stole over her face, a warmth found its way to her aching heart. For at last the love of seven years had found its way to her!

She felt all in a glad tumult as that perception came to her. It had, in truth, been an afternoon of revelations! She had never until now in the least understood Brian's character, never in the least appreciated him. And as to dreaming that his friendship had been love from the very first, it had never occurred to her.

The revelation did not bring her unalloyed happiness, for there came a sharp pang as she recollected what he had gone back to do. What if he should get into trouble on her behalf? what if he should be hurt? Accustomed always to fear for her father actual physical injury, her thoughts at once flew to the same danger for

Brian. But, however sick with anxiety, she was obliged, on reaching home, to try to copy out her article, which must be in type and upon thousands of breakfast-tables by the next morning, whether her heart ached or not, whether her life were rough or smooth.

In the meantime, Brian, having watched her cab drive off, turned back into Westminster Hall. He could see nothing but the one vision which filled his brain—the face of the girl he loved, a lovely, pure face suffused with tears. He could hear nothing but that intolerable slander which filled his heart with a burning, raging indignation. Straight as an arrow, and as if by instinct, he made his way to the place where Sir Algernon and three or four companions were pacing to and fro. He confronted them, bringing their walk to an enforced pause.

'I am here to demand an apology for the words you spoke just now about Miss Raeburn,' he said, speaking in a voice which was none the less impressive because it trembled slightly, as with a wrath restrained only by a great effort.

Sir Algernon, a florid, light-haired man of

about thirty, coolly stared at him for a moment.

'Who may you be, sir, who take up the cudgels so warmly in Miss Raeburn's defence?'

'A man who will not hear a defenceless girl insulted,' said Brian, his voice rising. 'Apologise!'

'Defenceless girl!' repeated the other, in a tone so insufferable that Brian's passion leapt up like wild-fire.

'You vile blackguard!' he cried, 'what you said was an infernal lie! and if you don't retract it this moment, I'll thrash you within an inch of your life!'

Sir Algernon laughed, and shrugged his shoulders.

''Pon my life!' he exclaimed, turning to one of his companions, 'if I'd known that Miss Raeburn——'

But the sentence was never ended, for with a look of fury Brian sprang at him, seized him by the collar of his coat, and holding him like a vice with one hand, with the other brought down his cane upon the slanderer's shoulders with such energy that the wretch writhed beneath it.

The onlookers being gentlemen, and fully aware that Sir Algernon deserved all he was getting, stood by not offering to interfere, perhaps in their hearts rather sympathising with the avenger, whose righteous indignation had about it a manliness that appealed to them. Presently Sir Algernon ceased to kick, his struggles grew fainter. Brian let his right arm pause then, and with his left flung his foe into the corner as if he had been a mere chattel.

'There!' he exclaimed, 'summons me for that when you please!' And, handing his card to one of Sir Algernon's companions, he strode out of the hall.

By the time he reached Guilford Square he was almost himself again, a little paler than usual, but outwardly quite calm. He went at once to No. 16. The Raeburns had now been settled in their new quarters for some weeks, and the house was familiar enough to him; he went up to the drawing-room, or as it was usually called the green-room. The gas was not lighted, but a little reading-lamp stood upon a table in one of the windows, and the firelight made the pannelled walls shine here and there, though the corners and recesses were all in dusky shadow. Erica had made this the most homelike room in the house; it had the most beguiling easy chairs, it had all Mr. Woodward's best pictures, it had fascinating little tables, and a tempting set of books. There was something in the sight of the familiar room which made Brian's wrath flame up once more. Erica's guileless life seemed to rise before him—the years of patient study, the beautiful filial love, the pathetic endeavour to restrain her child-like impatience of conventionalities, lest scandalmongers should have even a shadow of excuse for slandering Luke Raeburn's daughter. The brutality of the insult struck him more than ever. Erica, glancing up from her writing-table, saw that his face again bore that look of intolerable pain which had so greatly startled her in Westminster Hall.

She had more than half dreaded his arrival, had been wondering how they should meet after the strange revelation of the afternoon, had been thinking of the most trite and commonplace remark with which she might greet him. But when it actually came to the point she could not say a word, only looked up at him with eyes full of anxious questioning.

'It is all right,' he said, answering the mute question, a great joy thrilling him as he saw that she had been anxious about him. 'You should not have been afraid.'

'I couldn't help it,' she said, colouring, 'he is such a hateful man! a man who might do anything! Tell me what happened.'

'I gave him a thrashing which he'll not soon forget,' said Brian. 'But don't let us speak of him any more.'

'Perhaps he'll summons you!' said Erica.

'He won't dare to. He knows that he deserved it. What are you writing? you ought to be resting.'

'Only copying out my article. The boy will be here before long.'

'I am your doctor,' he said, feeling her pulse, and again assuming his authoritative manner; 'I shall order you to rest on your couch at once. I will copy this for you. What is it on?'

'Cremation,' said Erica, smiling a little. 'A nice funereal subject for a dreary day! Generally, if I'm in wild spirits, Mr. Bircham sends me the very gloomiest subject to write on, and, if I'm particularly blue, he asks for a bright, lively article.'

'Oh! he tells you what to write on?'

'Yes; did you think I had the luxury of choosing for myself? Every day, about eleven o'clock, a small boy brings me my fate on a slip of paper. Let me dictate this to you. I'm sure you can't read that pencilled scribble.'

'Yes, I can,' said Brian. 'You go and rest.'

She obeyed him, thankful enough to have a moment's pause in which to think out the questions that came crowding into her mind. She hardly dared to think what Brian might be to her, for just now she needed him so sorely as friend and adviser, that to admit that other perception, which made her feel shy and constrained with him, would have left her still in her isolation. After all, he was a seven years' friend, no mere acquaintance, but an actual friend to whom she was her unreserved and perfectly natural self.

'Brian,' she said, presently, when he had finished her copying, 'you don't think I'm bound to tell my father about this afternoon, do you?'

A burning, painful blush, the sort of blush that she never ought to have known, never could have known but for that shameful slander, spread over her face and neck as she spoke.

'Perhaps not,' said Brian, 'since the man has been properly punished.'

'I think—I hope it need never get round to him in any other way,' said Erica. 'He would be so fearfully angry, and just now scarcely a day passes without bringing him some fresh worry.'

'When will the Pogson affair come on?'

'Oh! I don't know. Not just yet, I'm afraid. Things in the legal world always move at the rate of a fly in a glue-pot.'

'What sort of man is Mr. Pogson?'

'He was in court to-day, a little, sleek, narrow-headed man, with cold, grey eyes. I have been trying to put myself in his place, and realise the view he takes of things; but it is very, very hard. You don't know what it is to live in this house and see the awful harm his intolerance is bringing about.'

'In what way did you specially mean?'

'Oh! in a thousand ways. It is bringing Christianity into discredit, it is making them more bitter against it, and who can wonder! It is bringing hundreds of men to atheism, it is enormously increasing the demand for all my father's books, and already even in these few months it has doubled the sale of the *Idol-Breaker*. In old times that would have been my consolation. Oh! it is heart-breaking to see how religious people injure their own cause! Surely they might have learnt by this time that punishment for opinion is never right, that it brings only bitterness, and misery, and more error! How is one to believe that this is right—that God means all this bigotry and injustice to go on producing evil?'

'Surely it will teach the sharp lesson that all pain teaches,' said Brian. 'We Christians have broken His order, have lost the true idea of brotherly love, and from this arises pain and evil, which at last, when it touches our own selfish natures, will rouse us, wake us up sharply, drive us back of necessity to the true Christ-following. Then persecution and injustice will die. But we are so terribly asleep that the evil must grow desperate before we become conscious of it. It seems to me that bigotry has at least one mortal foe, though. You are always here; you must show them by your life what the Father is—*that* is being a Christian!'

'I know,' said Erica, a look of almost passionate longing dawning in her eyes. 'Oh! what a thing it is to be crammed full of faults that hinder one from serving! And all these worries do try one's temper fearfully! If they had but a Donovan to live with them now! But, as for me, I can't do much, except love them.'

Brian loved her too truly to speak words of praise and commendation at such a time.

'Is not the love the crux of the whole?' he said, quietly.

'I suppose it is,' said Erica, pushing back the hair from her forehead in the way she always did when anything perplexed her. 'But just at present my life is a sort of fugue on Browning's line,

"How very hard it is to be a Christian!"

Sometimes I can't help laughing to think that there was a time when I thought the teaching of Christ unpractical! Do you mind ringing the bell for me; the others will be in directly, and will be glad of tea after that headachy place.'

'Is there nothing else I can do for you?' asked Brian.

'Yes, one more thing, help me to remember the levers of the second order. It's my physiology class to-night, and I feel, as Tom would express it, like a "boiled owl."'

'Let me take the class for you.'

'Oh, no, thank you,' she replied, 'I wouldn't miss it for the world.'

It was not till Brian had left that Erica, taking up the article on cremation, was struck by some resemblance in the handwriting. She must have seen Brian's writing before, but only this afternoon did she make that fresh discovery. Crossing the room she took from one of the book shelves a dark-blue morocco volume, and compared the writing on the fly-leaf with her MS.

'From another admirer of "Hiawatha."' There

could be no doubt that Brian had written that. Had he cared for her so long? Had he indeed loved her all these years? She was interrupted by the maid bringing in the tea.

'Mr. Bircham's boy is here, miss, and if you please can cook speak to you a minute?'

Erica put down the Longfellow and rolled up 'Cremation.'

'I'm sure she's going to give warning!' she thought to herself. 'What a day to choose for it! That's what I call an anti-climax.'

Her forebodings proved all too true. In a minute more in walked the cook, with the sort of conscious dignity of bearing which means—'I am no longer in your service.'

'If you please, miss, I wish to leave this day month.'

'I shall be sorry to lose you,' said Erica; 'what are your reasons for leaving?'

'I've not been used, miss, to families as is in the law-courts. I've been used to the best West-End private families.'

'I don't see how it can affect you,' said Erica, feeling, in spite of her annoyance, much inclined to laugh.

'Indeed, miss, and it do! There's not a tradesman's boy but has his joke or his word about Mr. Raeburn,' said the cook, in an injured voice. 'And last Sunday, when I went to the minister to show my lines, he said a member ought to be ashamed to take service with a hatheist, and that I was in an 'ouse of 'ell. Those was his very words, miss, an 'ouse of 'ell, he said.'

'Then it was exceedingly impertinent of him,' said Erica, 'for he knew nothing whatever about it.'

After that there was nothing for it but to accept the resignation and to begin once more the weary search for that rara avis, 'A good plain cook.'

Her interview had only just ended when she heard the front door open. She listened intently, but apparently it was only Tom; he came upstairs singing a refrain with which just then she quite agreed:—

'L A W,—law,
　Rhymes very well with jaw,
　If you're fond of litigation,
　And sweet procrastination,
　Latin and botheration,
　I advise you to go to law.'

'Hullo!' he exclaimed. 'So you did get home all right? I like your way of acting Casabianca! The chieftain sent me tearing out after you, and when I got there, you had vanished!'

'Brian came up just then,' said Erica, 'and I thought it better not to wait. Oh, here comes father.'

Raeburn entered as she spoke. No one who saw him would have guessed that he was an over-worked, over-worried man, for his face was a singularly peaceful one, serene with the serenity of a strong nature convinced of its own integrity.

'Got some tea for us, Eric?' he asked, throwing himself back in a chair beside the fire.

Some shade of trouble in her face, invisible to any eye but that of a parent, made him watch her intently, while a new hope which made his heart beat more quickly sprang up within him. Christians had not shown up well that day; prosecuting and persecuting Christians are the most repulsive beings on earth! Did she begin to feel a flaw in the system she had professed belief in? Might she by this injustice come to realise that she had unconsciously cheated herself into a belief? If such things might win her back to him, might bridge over that miserable gulf between them, then welcome any trouble, any persecution, welcome even ruin itself!

But had he been able to see into Erica's heart, he would have learnt that the grief which had left its traces on her face was the grief of knowing that such days as these strengthened and confirmed him in his atheism. Erica was indeed ever confronted with one of the most baffling of all baffling mysteries. How was it that a man of such grand capacities, a man with so many noble qualities, yet remained in the darkness? One day she put that question sadly enough to Charles Osmond.

'Not darkness, child, none of your honest Secularists who live up to their creed are in darkness,' he replied. 'However mistakenly, they do try to promote what they consider the general good. Were you in such absolute blackness before last summer?'

'There was the love of Humanity,' said Erica, musingly,

'Yes, and what is that but a ray of the light

of life promised to all who, to any extent, follow Christ? It is only the absolutely selfish who are in the black shadow. The honest atheist is in the penumbra, and in his twilight sees a little bit of the true sun, though he calls it Humanity instead of Christ.'

'Oh, if the shadows would but go!' exclaimed Erica.

'Would!' he said, laughing gently. 'Why, child, they will, they must!'

'But now, I mean! "Here down," as Mazzini would have said.'

'You were ever an impatient little mortal.'

'How can one help being impatient for this,' she said, with a quick sigh.

'That is what I used to say to myself seven years ago over you,' he said, smiling. 'But I learnt that the Father knew best, and that if we would work with Him we must wait with Him too. You mustn't waste your strength in impatience, child, you need every bit of it for the life before you.'

But patience did not come by nature to a Raeburn, and Erica did not gain it in a day even by grace.

## CHAPTER II.

#### FIESOLE.

And yet, because I love thee, I obtain
From that same love this vindicating grace,
To live on still in love, and yet in vain
To bless thee, yet renounce thee to thy face.
E. B. BROWNING.

MUCH has been said and written about the monotony of unalloyed pleasure, and the necessity of shadows and dark places in life as well as in pictured landscape. And certainly there can be but few, in this world of stern realities, who would dispute the fact that pleasure is doubled by its contrast with preceding pain. Perhaps it was the vividness of this contrast that made Raeburn and Erica enjoy, with a perfect rapture of enjoyment, a beautiful view and a beautiful spring day in Italy. Behind them lay a very sombre past; they had escaped for a brief moment from the atmosphere of strife, from the world of controversy, from the scorching breath of slander, from the baleful influences of persecution and injustice. Before them lay the fairest of all the cities of Italy. They were sitting in the Boboli gardens, and from the wooded heights looked down upon that loveliest of Italian valleys.

The silver Arno wound its way between the green encircling hills; then between the old houses of Florence, its waters spanned now by a light suspension-bridge—token of modern times—now by old brown arches strengthened and restored, now by the most venerable-looking of all the bridges, the Ponte Vecchio, with its double row of little shops. Into the cloudless blue sky rose the pinnacles of Santa Croce, the domes of San Spirito, of the Baptistery, of the Cathedral; sharply defined in the clear atmosphere were the airy, light Campanile of Giotto, the more slender brown tower of the Palazzo Vecchio, the spire of Santa Maria Novella. Northward, beyond the golden-brown city, rose the heights of Fiesole, and to the east the green hills, dotted all over with white houses, swept away into the unseen distance.

Raeburn had been selected as the English delegate to attend a certain political gathering held that year at Florence. He had at first hesitated to accept the post, for his work at home had enormously increased; but the long months of wearing anxiety had so told upon him, that his friends had at length persuaded him to go, fully aware that the only chance of inducing him to take any rest was to get him out of the region of work.

The 'Miracles' trial was at length over, but Mr. Pogson had not obtained the desire of his heart, namely, the imprisonment and fining of Luke Raeburn. The only results of the trial were the extensive advertisement of the pamphlet in question, a great increase of bitterness on each side, and a great waste of money. Erica's sole consolation lay in the fact that a few of the more liberal thinkers were beginning to see the evil, and to agitate for a repeal of the Blasphemy Laws. As for the action for libel, there was no chance of its coming on before June, and in the meantime Mr. Pogson's letter was obtaining a wider circulation, and perhaps, on the whole, Luke Raeburn was just at that time the best-abused man in all England.

There had been a long silence between the father and daughter, who understood each other far too well to need many words at such a time; but at length a sudden ejaculation from Raeburn made Erica turn her eyes from Fiesole to the shady walk in the gardens down which he was looking.

'Does any Italian walk at such a pace?' he exclaimed. 'That must surely be Brian Osmond, or his double in the shape of an English tourist.'

'Oh, impossible!' said Erica, colouring a little, and looking intently at the pedestrian, who was still at some little distance.

'But it is,' said Raeburn—'height, way of walking, everything! My dear Eric, don't tell me I can't recognise the man who saved my life. I should know him a mile off!'

'What can have brought him here?' said Erica, a certain joyous tumult in her heart checked by the dread of evil tidings—a dread which was but natural to one who had lived her life.

'Come and meet him,' said Raeburn. 'Ha, Brian, I recognised you ever so far off, and couldn't persuade this child of your identity.'

Brian, a little flushed with quick walking, looked up into Erica's face searchingly, and was satisfied with what he read there—satisfied with the soft glow of colour that came to her cheeks, and with the bright look of happiness that came into her eyes, which, as a rule, were grave, and when in repose even sad in expression.

'I owe this to a most considerate patient, who thought fit to be taken ill at Genoa and to telegraph for me,' he said, in explanation; 'and being in Italy, I thought I might as well take my yearly outing now.'

'Capital idea!' said Raeburn. 'You are the very man we wanted. What with meetings and interviews, I don't get much peace even here, and Erica is much in need of an escort sometimes. How did you find us?'

'They told me at the hotel that I should probably find you here, though, if I had known what a wilderness of a place it is, I should have been rather hopeless.'

Erica left most of the talking to her father; just then she felt no wish to put a single thought into words. She wanted only to enjoy the blissful, dream-like happiness, which was so new, and rare, and wonderful that it brought with it the feeling that any very definite thought or word must bring it to an end. Perfect harmony with your surroundings! Yes, that was indeed a very true definition of happiness; and of late the surroundings had been so grim and stormy! She seemed to tread upon air as they roamed about the lovely walks. The long, green vistas were to her a veritable paradise. Her father looked so happy, too, and had so entirely shaken off his cares, and Brian, who was usually rather silent, seemed to-day a perfect fountain of talk.

Since that December day in Westminster Hall, a great change had come over Erica. Not a soul besides Brian and herself knew anything about the scene with Sir Algernon Wyte. Not a word had passed between them since upon the subject; but perhaps, because of the silence, that day was all the more in the thoughts of each. The revelation of Brian's love revealed also to Erica much in his character which had hitherto perplexed her, simply because she had not seen it in the true light. There had always been about him a wistfulness bordering on sadness, which had sometimes almost angered her. For so little do even intimate friends know each other, that lives, which seem all peaceful and full of everything calculated to bring happiness, are often the ones which are preyed upon by some grievous trouble or anxiety unknown to any outsider. If he had indeed loved her all those seven years, he must have suffered fearfully. What the suffering had been, Erica could, from her present position, understand well enough. The thought of it touched her inexpressibly, seemed to her, as indeed it was, the shadow of that Divine Love which had loved her eternally—had waited for her through long years—had served her and shielded her, though she never recognised its existence, till at length, in one flash of light, the revelation had come to her, and she had learnt the glory of Love, the murky gloom of those past misunderstandings.

Those were wonderful days that they spent

together at Florence, the sort of days that come but once in a life-time; for the joy of dawn is quite distinct from the bright noonday or the calm evening, distinct, too, from that second and grander dawn which awaits us in the Unseen when the night of life is over. Together they wandered through the long corridors of the Uffizzi; together they returned again and again to the Tribune, or traversed that interminable passage across the river which leads to the Pitti Gallery, or roamed about among the old squares and palaces, which are haunted by so many memories. And every day Brian meant to speak, but could not, because the peace, and restfulness, and glamour of the present was so perfect, and perhaps because, unconsciously, he felt that these were 'halcyon days.'

On Sunday he made up his mind that he certainly would speak before the day was over. He went with Erica to see the old monastery of San Marco before morning service at the English church. But, though they were alone together, he could not bring himself to speak there. They wandered from cell to cell, looking at those wonderful frescoes of the Crucifixion, in each of which Fra Angelico seemed to gain some fresh thought, some new view of his inexhaustible subject. And Brian, watching Erica, thought how that old master would have delighted in the pure face and perfect colouring, in the short auburn hair, which was in itself a halo, but could not somehow just then draw her thoughts away from the frescoes. Together they stood in the little cells occupied once by Savonarola; looked at the strange, stern face which Bastianini chiselled so effectively; stood by the old wooden desk where Savonarola had written and read, saying very little to one another, but each conscious that the silence was one of perfect understanding and sympathy. Then came the service in a hideous church, which yet seemed beautiful to them, with indifferent singing, which was somehow sweeter to them than the singing of a trained choir elsewhere.

But, on returning to the hotel, Brian found that his chances for that day were over, for all the afternoon Erica had to receive a constant succession of visitors, who, as she said, turned her father for the time being into the 'British lion.' In the evening, too, when they walked in the Cascine, they were no longer alone. Raeburn went with them, and as they paced along the broad avenue with the Arno gleaming through the fresh green of the trees, talking of the discussions of the past week, he inadvertently touched the note of pain in an otherwise cloudless day.

'The work is practically over now,' he said. 'But I think I must take a day or two to see a little of Florence. I must be at Salzburg to meet Hasenbalg by Wednesday week. Can you be ready to leave here on Wednesday, Eric?'

'Oh! yes, father,' she said, without hesitation or comment, but with something in her voice which told Brian that she, too, felt a pang of regret at the thought that their days in that city of golden dreams were so soon to be ended.

The Monday morning, however, proved so perfect a day that it dispelled the shadow that had fallen on them. Raeburn wished to go to Fiesole, and early in the morning, Brian having secured a carriage and settled the terms with the crafty-looking Italian driver, they set off together. The sunny streets looked sunnier than ever; the Tornabuoni was as usual lively and bustling; the flower-market at the base of the Palazzo Strozzi was gay with pinks and carnations and early roses. They drove out of the city, past innumerable villas, out into the open country, where the only blot upon the fair landscape was a funeral train, the coffin borne by those gruesome beings, the Brothers of the Misericordia, with their black robes and black face-cloths pierced only with holes for the eyes.

'Is it necessary to make death so repulsive?' said Raeburn. 'Our own black hearses are bad enough, but upon my word I should be sorry to be carried to my grave by such grim beings!'

He took off his hat, however, as they passed, and that not merely out of deference to the custom of the country, but because of the deep reverence with which he invariably regarded the dead—a reverence which in his own country was marked by the involuntary softening of his voice when he alluded to the death of others, the token of a nature which, though strangely twisted, was in truth deeply reverential.

Then began the long ascent, the road, as usual, being lined with beggars, who importunately followed the carriage; while, no sooner had they reached the village itself, than they were besieged by at least a dozen women selling the straw baskets which are the speciality of Fiesole.

'*Ecco, signor! ecco, signorina!* Vary sheep! vary sheep!' resounded on all sides, each vendor thrusting her wares forward, so that progress was impossible.

'What a plague this is!' said Raeburn. 'They'll never leave you in peace, Erica; they are too well used to the soft-hearted *signorina Inglese.*'

'Well, then, I shall leave you to settle them,' said Erica, laughing, 'and see if I can't sketch a little in the amphitheatre. They can't torment us there, because there is an entrance fee.'

'All right; and I will try this bird's-eye view of Florence,' said Raeburn, establishing himself upon the seat which stands on the verge of the hill looking southward. He was very fond of making pen-and-ink sketches, and by his determined, though perfectly courteous manner, he at last succeeded in dismissing the basket-women.

Erica and Brian, in the meantime, walked down the steep little path which leads back to the village, on their way encountering a second procession of Brothers bearing a coffin. In a few minutes they had found their way into a quiet garden, at the remote end of which, far from the houses of Fiesole, and sheltered on all sides by the green Appenines, was an old Roman amphitheatre. Grass and flowers had sprung up now on the arena where, in olden times, had been fearful struggles between men and beasts. Wild roses and honeysuckle drooped over the grey old building, and in between the great blocks of stone which formed the tiers of seats for the spectators, sprang the yellow celandine and the white star of Bethlehem.

Erica sat down upon one of the stony seats, and began to sketch the outline of the hills, and roughly to draw in the foreground the further side of the amphitheatre and a broken column which lay in the middle.

'Would you mind fetching me some water?' she said to Brian.

There was a little trickling stream close by, half hidden by bramble bushes. Brian filled her glass, and watched her brush as she washed in the sky.

'Is that too blue, do you think?' she asked, glancing up at him with one of her bright looks.

'Nothing could be too deep for such a sky as this,' he replied, half absently. Then, with a sudden change of tone, 'Erica, do you remember the first day you spoke to me.'

'Under murky London skies very unlike these,' she said, laughing a little, but nervously. 'You mean the day when our umbrellas collided!'

'You mustn't abuse the murky skies,' said Brian, smiling. 'If the sun had been shining, the collision would never have occurred. Oh, Erica! what a lifetime it seems since that day in Gower Street! I little thought then that I should have to wait more than seven years to tell you of my love, or that at last I should tell you in a Roman amphitheatre under these blue skies. Erica, I think you have known it of late. Have you, my darling? Have you known how I loved you?'

'Yes,' she said, looking down at her sketch-book with glowing cheeks.

'Oh! if you knew what a paradise of hope you opened to me that day last December, and how different life has been ever since! Those were grey years, Erica, when I dared not even hope to gain your love. But lately, darling, I have hoped. Was I wrong?'

'No,' she said, with a little quiver in her voice.

'You will love me?'

She looked up at him for a moment in silence, a glorious light in her golden brown eyes, her whole face radiant with joy.

'I do love you,' she said, softly.

He drew nearer to her, held both her hands in his, waiting only for the promise which would make her, indeed, his own.

'Will you be my wife, darling?'

But the words had scarcely passed his lips when a look of anguish swept over Erica's face; she snatched away her hands.

'Oh! God help me!' she cried. 'What have I done? I've been living in a dream! It's impossible, Brian! Impossible!'

A grey look came over Brian's face.

'How impossible?' he asked, in a choked voice.

'I can't leave home,' she said, clasping her hands tightly together. 'I never can leave my father.'

'I will wait,' said Brian, recovering his voice, 'I will wait any time for you—only give me hope.'

'I can't,' she sobbed. 'I daren't!'

'But you have given it me!' he exclaimed. 'You have said you loved me!'

'I do! I do!' she cried, passionately. 'But, oh, Brian! have pity on me—don't make me say it again—I must not think of it—I can never be your wife.'

Her words were broken with sobs, which she could not restrain.

'My darling,' he said, growing calm and strong again at the sight of her agitation, and once more possessing himself of her hand, ' you have had a great many troubles lately, and I can quite understand that just now you could not leave your father. But I will wait till less troubled times; then surely you will come to me?'

'No,' she said, quickly, as if not daring to pause, 'it will always be the same; there never will be quiet times for us. I can't leave my father! It isn't as if he had other children—I am the only one, and I must stay.'

'Is this, then, to be the end of it all?' cried Brian. 'My darling, you cannot be so cruel to me! It cannot be the end—there is no end to love—and we know that we love each other. Erica, give me some future to look to—some hope!'

The terrible pain expressed in every line of his face wrung her heart.

'Oh, wait,' she exclaimed. 'Give me one moment to think.'

She buried her face in her hands, shutting out the sunny Italian landscape, the very beauty of which seemed to weaken her powers of endurance. Truly she had been living lately in a golden dream, and the waking was anguish. Oh, if she had but realised before the meaning of it all, then she would have hidden her love so that he never would have guessed it! She would have been to him the Erica of a year ago, just a friend and nothing more! But now she must give him the worst of pain, perhaps ruin his whole life! If she might but give him some promise! What was the right? How were love and duty to be reconciled?

As she sat crouched up in her misery, fighting the hardest battle of her life, the bell in the campanile of the village church began to ring. It was twelve o'clock. All through the land, in remembrance of the hour when the true meaning of love and sacrifice was revealed to the human race, there swept now the music of church-bells, bidding the people to pause in their work and pray. Many a peasant raised his thoughts for a moment from sordid cares or hard labour, and realised that there was an unseen world. And here in the Roman amphitheatre, where a conflict more painful than those physical conflicts of old time was going on, a soul prayed in agony for the wisdom to see the right and the strength to do it.

When at length Erica lifted her face, she found that Brian was no longer beside her, he was pacing to and fro in the arena; the waiting had grown unbearable to him. She went down to him, moving neither quickly nor hurriedly, but at the steady, 'right onward' pace which suited her whole aspect.

'Brian,' she said, in a low voice, 'do you remember telling me that day that I must try to show them what the Father is? You must help me now, not hinder. You will help me just because you do indeed love me!'

'You will give me no promise even for the most distant future?'

'I can't,' she replied, faltering a little as she saw him turn deadly white. 'If there were any engagement between us, I should have to tell my father of it, and that would only make our trouble his and defeat my whole object. Oh, Brian, forgive me, and just leave me. I can have given you nothing but pain all these years. Don't let me spoil your whole life!'

His face caught something of the noble purpose which made hers shine in spite of the sadness.

'Darling,' he said, quickly, 'I can thank God for you, though you are never to be mine. God bless you, Erica.'

There was a moment's pause; he still kept her hands in his.

'Tell your father I've gone for a walk, over to those hills—that I shall not be home till evening.' He felt her hands tremble, and knew that he only tortured her by staying. 'Will you kiss me once, Erica?' he said.

She lifted a pale steadfast face and quivering lips to his, and after that one long embrace they parted. When he turned away, Erica stood quite still for a minute in the arena listening to his retreating footsteps. Her heart, which had throbbed painfully, seemed now only to echo his steps, to beat more faintly as they grew less audible. At last came silence, and then she crept up to the place where she had left her sketch-book and paint-box.

The whole world seemed sliding away—aching desolation overwhelmed her. Brian's face with its passion and pain rose before her dry, burning eyes. Then darkness came, blotting out the sunshine; the little stream trickling into its stony basin seemed to grow into a roaring cataract, the waters to rush into her ears with a horrid gurgling; while the stones of the amphitheatre seemed to change into blocks of ice and to freeze her as she lay.

A few minutes later she gasped her way painfully back to life. All was very peaceful now; the water fell with its soft tinkling sound, there was a low hum of insects; beside her stony pillow grew some stars of Bethlehem, and in between their delicate white and green she could see the arena and the tiers of seats opposite, and out beyond the green encircling hills. Golden sunshine lighted up the dark pines and spire-like cypresses; in the distance there was an olive-garden, its soft, grey-green foliage touched into silvery brightness.

The beauty of the scene, which in her struggle had seemed to weaken and unnerve her, stole now into her heart and comforted her; and all the time there rang in her ears the message that the bells had brought her,—'Who for the joy that was set before Him, endured the cross.'

'Taking a siesta?' said a voice above her. She looked up and saw her father.

'I've rather a headache,' she replied.

'Enough to give you one, my child, to lie there in the sun without an umbrella,' he said, putting up his own to shelter her. 'Such a May noon-day in Italy might give you a sun-stroke. What was your doctor thinking of to allow it?'

'Brian? Oh, he has gone over to those hills; we are not to wait for him, he wanted a walk.'

'Quite right,' said Raeburn. 'I don't think he ought to waste his holiday in Italian cities, he wants fresh air and exercise after his London life. Where's your handkerchief?'

He took it to the little stream, put aside the overhanging bushes, dipped it in the water, and bringing it back laid it on her burning forehead.

'How you spoil me, *padre mio*,' she said, with a little laugh that was sadder than tears; and as she spoke she slipped down to a lower step and rested her head on his knee, drawing down one of his strong hands to shade her eyes. He talked of his sketch, of his word-skirmish with the basket-women, of the view from the amphitheatre; but she did not much hear what he said, she was looking at the hand that shaded her eyes. That strong hand which had toiled for her when she was a helpless baby, the hand to which she had clung when every other support had been wrenched away by death, the hand which she had held in hers when she thought he was dying, and the children had sung of 'Life's long day and death's dark night.'

All at once she drew it down and pressed it to her lips with a child's loving reverence. Then she sat up with a sudden return of energy.

'There, now let us go home,' she exclaimed. 'My head aches a little still, but we won't let it spoil our last day but one in Florence. Didn't we talk of San Miniato for this afternoon?'

It was something of a relief to find, on returning, an invitation to dinner for that evening which Raeburn could not well refuse. Erica kept up bravely through the afternoon, but when she was once more alone her physical powers gave way. She was lying on her bed sick and faint and weary, and with the peculiarly desolate feeling which comes to most people when they are ill in a hotel with all the unheeding bustle going on around them. There came a knock at her door.

'*Entrate*,' she said, quickly, welcoming any

fresh voice which would divert her mind from the weary longing for her mother. A sort of wild hope sprang up within her that some woman friend would be sent to her, that Gladys Farrant, or old Mrs. Osmond, or her secularist friend Mrs. MacNaughton, whom she loved best of all, would suddenly find themselves in Florence and come to her in her need.

There entered a tall, over-worked waiter. He looked first at her, then at the note in his hand, spelling out the direction with a puzzled face.

'Mees Rabi—Rabi—Rabi—Rabi—an?' he asked, hesitatingly.

'*Grazie*,' she replied, almost snatching it from him. The colour rushed to her cheeks as she saw the writing was Brian's, and the instant the waiter had closed the door, she tore open the envelope with trembling hands.

It was a last appeal, written after he had returned from wandering among the Appenines, worn out in body, and shaken from the noble fortitude of the morning. The strong passionate words woke an answering thrill in Erica's heart. He asked her to think it all over once more, he had gone away too hastily. If she could change her mind, could see any possible hope for the future, would she write to him? If he heard nothing from her, he would understand what the silence meant. This was in brief the substance of the letter, but the words had a passionate, unrestrained intensity which showed they had been written by a man of strong nature overwrought by suffering and excitement.

He was here, in the very hotel! Might she not write to him?—might she not send him some sort of message—write just a word of indefinite hope which would comfort and relieve herself as well as him? 'If I do not hear from you, I shall understand what your silence means.' Ah! but would he understand? What had she said this morning to him? Scarcely anything—the merest broken bits of sentences, the poorest, coldest confession of love.

Her writing-case lay open on the table beside the bed, with an unfinished letter to Aunt Jean, begun before they had started for Fiesole. She snatched up paper and pen, and, trembling so much that she could scarcely support herself, she wrote two brief lines.

'Darling, I love you, and always must love you, first and best.'

Then she lay back again exhausted, looking at the poor little weak words, which would not contain a thousandth part of the love in her heart. Yet, though the words were true, would they perhaps convey a wrong meaning to him? Ought she to send them? On the other hand, would he indeed understand the silence—the silence which seemed now intolerable to her? She folded the note and directed it, the tumult in her heart growing wilder as she did so. Once more there raged the battle which she had fought in the amphitheatre that morning, and she was not so strong now; she was weakened by physical pain, and to endure was far harder. It seemed to her that her whole life would be unbearable if she did not send him that message. And to send it was so fatally easy; she had merely to ring, and then in a few minutes the note would be in his hands.

It was a little narrow slip of a room; all her life long she could vividly recall it. The single bed pushed close to the wall, the writing-table with its gay-patterned cloth, the hanging wardrobe with glass doors, the walls trellised with roses, and on the ceiling a painting of some white swans eternally swimming in an ultramarine lake. The window, unshuttered, but veiled by muslin curtains, looked out upon the Arno ; from her bed she could see the lights on the further bank. On the wall close beside her was a little round wooden projection. If it had been a rattlesnake, she could not have gazed at it more fixedly. Then she looked at the printed card above, and the words written in French and English, German and Italian, seemed to fall mechanically on her brain, though burning thoughts seethed there too.

'Ring once for hot water, twice for the chambermaid, three times for the waiter.'

Merely to touch that ivory knob, and then by the lightest pressure of the finger-tips a whole world of love and happiness and rest might open for her, and life would be changed for ever.

Again and again she was on the point of yielding, but each time she resisted, and each resistance made her stronger. At length, with a fearful effort, she turned her face away and buried it in the pillow, clinging with all her might to the iron-work of the bed.

For at least an hour—the most frightful hour of her life—she did not dare to stir. At last, when her hands were stiff and sore with that rigid grasping, when it seemed as if her heart had been wrenched out of her, and had left nothing but an aching void, she sat up and tore both Brian's note and her reply into a thousand pieces; then, in a weary, lifeless way, made her preparations for the night.

But sleep was impossible. The struggle was over for ever, but the pain was but just begun, and she was still a young girl, with the best part of life stretching out before her. She did not toss about restlessly, but lay very still, just enduring her misery, while all the every-day sounds came to her from without—laughter in the next room from two talkative American girls, doors opening and shutting, boots thrown down, electric bells rung, presently her father's step and voice.

'Has Miss Raeburn been up long?'

'Sairtenlee, sair, yes,' replied the English-speaking waiter. 'The *signorina* sleeps, doubtless.'

Then came a pause, and in another minute her father's door was closed and locked.

Noisy parties of men shouting out some chorus sung at one of the theatres passed along the Lung' Arno, and twanging mandolins wandered up and down in the moonlight. The sound of that harshest and most jarring of all musical instruments was ever after hateful to her. She could not hear one played without a shudder.

Slowly and wearily the night wore on. Sometimes she stole to the window and looked out on the sleeping city, on the peaceful Arno which was bathed in silvery moonlight, and on the old, irregular houses, thinking what struggles and agonies this place had witnessed in past times, and realising what an infinitesimal bit of the world's sufferings she was called to bear. Sometimes she lit a candle and read, sometimes prayed, but for the most part just lay still, silently enduring, learning, though she did not think it, the true meaning of pain.

Somewhat later than usual, she joined her father the next morning in the coffee-room.

'Brian tells me he is off to-day,' was Raeburn's greeting. 'It seems that he must see that patient at Genoa again, and he wants to get a clear fortnight in Switzerland.'

'Is it not rather early for Switzerland?'

'I should have thought so; but he knows more about it than I do. He has written to try to persuade your friend, Mr. Farrant, to join him in the Whitsuntide recess.'

'Oh, I am glad of that,' said Erica, greatly relieved.

Directly after breakfast she went out with her father, going first of all to French's bank, where Raeburn had to change a circular note.

'It is upstairs,' he said, as they reached the house. 'Don't you trouble to come up; you'll have stairs enough presently at the Uffizzi.'

'Very well,' she replied, 'I will wait for you here.'

She stood in the doorway, looking out thoughtfully at the busy Tornabuoni and its gay shops; but in a minute a step she knew sounded on the staircase, and the colour rushed to her cheeks.

'I have just said good-bye to your father,' said Brian. 'I am leaving Florence this morning. You must forgive me for having written last night. I ought not to have done it, and I understood your silence.'

He spoke calmly, in the repressed voice of a man who holds 'passion in a leash.' Erica was thankful to have the last sight of him thus— calm and strong and self-restrained. It was a nobler side of love than that which had inspired his letter—nobler because freer from thought of self.

'I am so glad you will have Donovan,' she said. 'Good-bye.'

He took her hand in his, pressed it, and turned away without a word.

## CHAPTER III.

### 'RIGHT ONWARD.'

> Therefore my Hope arose
> From out her swound and gazed upon Thy face,
> And, meeting there that soft subduing look
> Which Peter's spirit shook,
> Sank downward in a rapture to embrace
> Thy pierced hands and feet with kisses close,
> And prayed Thee to assist her evermore
> To 'reach the things before.'
> E. B. BROWNING.

'I'M really thankful it is the last time I shall have to get this abominable paper money,' said Raeburn, coming down the stairs. 'Just count these twos and fives for me, dear; fifteen of each there should be.'

At that moment Brian had just passed the tall, white column, disappearing into the street which leads to the Borgo Ogni Santi. Erica turned to begin her new chapter of life heavily handicapped in the race, for once more that deadly faintness crept over her, a numbing, stifling pressure, as if Pain in physical form had seized her heart in his cold clasp. But with all her strength she fought against it, forcing herself to count the hateful little bits of paper, and thankful that her father was too much taken up with the arrangement of his purse to notice her.

'I'm glad we happened to meet Brian,' he remarked; 'he goes by an earlier train than I thought. Now, little son Eric, where shall we go? We'll have a day of unmitigated pleasure and throw care to the winds. I'll even forswear Vieusseux; there won't be much news to-day.'

'Let us take the Pitti Palace first,' said Erica, knowing that the fresh air and the walk would be the only chance for her.

She walked very quickly, with the feeling that, if she were still for a single moment, she should fall down. And, luckily, Raeburn thought her paleness accounted for by yesterday's headache and the wakeful night, and never suspected the true state of the case. On they went past fascinating marble shops and jewellers' windows filled with Florentine mosaics, across the Ponte

Vecchio, down a shady street, and into the rough-hewn, grim-looking palace. It was to Erica like a dream of pain; the surroundings were so lovely, the sunshine so perfect, and her own heart so sore.

But within that old palace she found the true cure for sore hearts. She remembered having looked with Brian at an 'Ecce Homo,' by Carlo Dolci, and thought she would like to see it again. It was not a picture her father would have cared for, and she left him looking at Raphael's 'Three Ages of Man,' and went by herself into the little room which is called the 'Hall of Ulysses.' The picture was a small one, and had what are considered the usual faults of the painter, but it was the first 'Ecce Homo' that Erica had ever cared for; and, whatever the shortcomings of the execution, the ideal was a most beautiful one. The traces of physical pain were not brought into undue prominence, appearing not at all in the face, which was full of unutterable calm and dignity. The deep, brown eyes had the strange power which belongs to some pictures, they followed you all over the room—there was no escaping them.

They were hauntingly sad eyes, eyes in which there lurked grief unspeakable; not the grief which attends bodily pain, but the grief which grieves for others—the grief which grieves for humanity, for its thousand ills and ignorances, its doubts and denials, its sins and sufferings. There was no bitterness in it, no restlessness, no questioning. It was the grief of a noble, strong man whose heart is torn by the thought of the sin and misery of his brothers, but who knows that the Father can, and will, turn the evil into the means of glorious gain.

As Erica looked, the true meaning of pain seemed to flash upon her. Dimly she had apprehended it in the days of her atheism, had clung to the hope that the pain of the few brought the gain of the many; but now the hope became certainty, the faith became open vision. For was it not all here, written in clearest characters, in the life of the Ideal Man? And is not what was true for him, true for us, too? We talk much about 'Christ our example,' and struggle painfully along the uphill road of the 'Imitation of Christ,' meaning by that too often a vague endeavour to be 'good,' to be patient, to be not entirely absorbed in the things which are seen. But when pain comes, when the immense misery and evil in the world are borne in upon us, we too often stumble, or fail utterly, just because we do not understand our sonship; because we forget that Christians must be sin-bearers like their Master, pain-bearers like their Master; because we will let ourselves be blinded by the mystery of evil and the mystery of pain, instead of fixing our eyes, as Christ did, on the joy that those mysteries are sure to bring. 'Lo, I come to do Thy will.' And what is the will of even a good earthly father but the best possible for all his children?

Erica saw for the first time that no pain she had ever suffered had been a wasted thing, nor had it merely taught her personally some needful lesson; it had been rather her allotted service, her share of pain-bearing, sin-bearing, Christ-following; her opportunity of doing the 'Will'—not self-chosen, but given to her as one of the best of gifts by the Father himself.

'Oh, what a little fool I've been!' she thought to herself, with the strange pang of joy which comes when we make some discovery which sweetens the whole of life, and which seems so self-evident that we can but wonder and wonder at our dense stupidity in not seeing it sooner. 'I've been grudging Brian what God sees he most wants! I've been groaning over the libels and injustices which seem to bring so much pain and evil, when, after all, they will be, in the long run, the very things to show people the need of tolerance, and to establish freedom of speech.'

Even this pain of renunciation seemed to gain a new meaning for her, though she could not in the least fathom it; even the unspeakable grief of feeling that her father was devoting much of his life to the propagation of error, lost its bitterness, though it retained its depth. For with the true realisation of Fatherhood and Sonship impatience and bitterness die, and in their place rises the peace which 'passeth understanding.'

'We will have a day of unmitigated pleasure,' her father had said to her, and the words had at the time been like a sharp stab. But, after all, might not this pain, this unseen and dimly understood work for humanity, be in very truth the truest pleasure? What artist is there who would not gratefully receive from the Master an order to attempt the loftiest of subjects? What poet is there whose heart would not bound when he knew he was called to write on the noblest of themes? All the struggles, all the weary days of failure, all the misery of conscious incompleteness, all the agony of soul—these were but means to the end, and so inseparably bound up with the end that they were no more evil but good, their darkness overflooded with the light of the work achieved.

Raeburn, coming into the room, saw what she was looking at, and turned away. Little as he could understand her thoughts, he was not the sort of man to wound unnecessarily one who differed from him. His words in public were sharp and uncompromising: in debate he did not much care how he hit as long as he hit hard. But, apart from the excitement of such sword-play, he was, when convinced that his hearers were honest Christians, genuinely sorry to give them pain.

Erica found him looking at a Sèvres china

vase in which he could not by any possibility have been interested.

'I feel Mr. Ruskin's wrathful eye upon me,' she said, laughing, 'Now, after spending all that time before a Carlo Dolci, we must really go to the Uffizzi and look at Botticelli's "Fortitude." Brian and I nearly quarrelled over it the last time we were there.'

So they wandered away together through the long galleries, Erica pointing out her favourite pictures and hearing his opinion about them. And indeed Raeburn was as good a companion as could be wished for in a picture-gallery. The intense development of the critical faculty, which had really been the bane of his existence, came here to his aid, for he had a quick eye for all that was beautiful both in art and nature, and wonderfully keen powers of observation. The refreshment, too, of leaving for a moment his life of excessive toil was great; Erica hoped that he really did find the day, for once, 'unmitigated pleasure.'

They went to Santa Croce, they walked through the crowded market, they had a merry dispute about ascending the Campanile.

'Just this one you really must let me try,' said Erica, 'they say it is very easy.'

'To people without spines, perhaps it may be,' said Raeburn.

'But think of the view from the top,' said Erica, 'and it really won't hurt me. Now, *padre mio*, I'm sure it's for the greatest happiness of the greatest number that I should go up!'

'It's the old story,' said Raeburn smiling,

" "Vain is the hope, by any force or skill,
To stem the current of a woman's will;
For if she will, she will, you may depend on't,
And if she won't, she won't, and there's an end on't."

However, since this is probably the last time in our lives that we shall have the chance, perhaps, I'll not do the tyrannical father.'

They had soon climbed the steep staircase, and were quite rewarded by the magnificent view from the top, a grand panorama of city and river and green Appenines. Erica looked northward to Fiesole with a fast-throbbing heart. Yet it seemed as if half a lifetime lay between the passion-tossed yesterday and the sad yet peaceful present. Nor was the feeling a mere delusion; she had indeed in those brief hours lived years of the spirit life.

She did not stay long at that northern parapet; thoughts of her own life or even of Brian's would not do just then. She had to think of her father, to devote herself to him. And somehow, though her heart was sad, yet her happiness was real, as they tried together to make out the various buildings; and her talk was unrestrained, and even her laughter natural, not forced; for it is possible to those who really love to throw themselves altogether into the life of another, and to lay aside all thought of self.

Once or twice that day she half feared that her father must guess all that had happened. He was so very careful of her, so considerate; and for Raeburn to be more considerate meant a great deal, for in private he was always the most gentle man imaginable. His opponents, who often regarded him as a sort of 'fiend in human shape,' were strangely mistaken in their estimate of his character. When treated with discourtesy or unfairness in public, it was true that he hit back again, and hit hard; and, since even in the nineteenth century we are so foolish as to use these weapons against the expression of opinions we deem mischievous, Raeburn had had a great deal of practice in this retaliation. He was a very proud and a very sensitive man, not blessed with overmuch patience. But he held his opinions honestly, and had suffered much for them; he had a real love for humanity, and an almost passionate desire to better his generation. To such a man it was no light thing to be deemed everything that is vile; like poor Shelley, he found it exceedingly bitter to let 'murderers and traitors take precedence of him in public opinion.' People in general took into account all his harsh utterances (and some of them were very harsh), but they rarely thought anything about the provocation received, the excessively hard life that this man had lived, the gross personal insults which he had had to put up with, the galling injustice he had had to fight against. Upon this side of the question they just turned their backs, pooh-poohed it, or, when it was forced upon their notice, said (unanswerable argument!) 'It couldn't be so!'

When, as they were making the descent, Erica found the strong hand stretched out for hers the moment the way grew dark, when she was warned of the slightest difficulty by, 'Take care, little one, a narrow step,' or, ''Tis rather broken here,' she almost trembled to think that, in spite of all her efforts, he might have learnt how matters really were. But by-and-by his serenity re-assured her.; had he thought that she was in trouble, his face would not have been so cloudless.

And in truth Raeburn, spite of his keen observation, never thought for a moment of the true state of the case. He was a very literal, unimaginative man, and, having once learnt to regard Brian as an old family friend and as his doctor, he never dreamed of regarding him in the light of his daughter's lover. Also, as is not unfrequently the case when a man has only one child, he never could take-in the fact that she was quite grown up. Even when he read her articles in the *Daily Review*, or discussed the most weighty topics with her, she was always 'little son Eric,' or his 'little one.' And Erica's unquenchable high spirits served to keep up the delusion. She would as often as not end a conversation on Darwinism by a romp with

Friskarina, or write a very thoughtful article on *Scrutin de Liste*, and then spring up from her desk and play like any child with an india-rubber ball nominally kept for children visitors.

She managed to tide over those days bravely and even cheerfully for her father's sake. It was easier when they had left Florence, with its over-bright and over-sad memories. Peaceful old Verona was more in accordance with her state of mind; and from thence they went to Trento, and over the Brenner, passing Botzen and Brixen in their lovely valley, gaining a brief glimpse of the spire-like Dolomites, and gradually ascending the pass, leaving the river and its yellow reeds, and passing through the rich pasture-land, where the fields were bright with buttercups and daisies—gold and silver of the people's property, as Raeburn called them. Then on once more between crimson and purple porphyry mountains, nearer and nearer to the snowy mountain peaks; and at last, as the day drew to an end, they descended again, and saw down below them, in the loveliest of valleys, a little town, its white houses suffused by a crimson sunset glow.

'Innsbruck, madam, Innsbruck!' said a fat old Tyrolese man, who had been showing them all the beauties of his beloved country throughout the journey.

And, though nothing could ever again have for Erica the sweet glamour of an Italian city, yet she was glad now to have seen the last of that sunny land, and welcomed the homely little place with its matter-of-fact houses and prosperous comfort. She felt, somehow, that it would be easier to endure now that she was fairly out of Italy.

The day after their arrival in Innsbruck was Sunday. There was no English service as yet, for the season had not begun, but Erica went to the little Lutheran church, and Raeburn, who had never been to a Lutheran service, went with her, for the sake of studying the congregation, the preacher, and the doctrine. Also, perhaps, because he did not want her to feel lonely in a foreign place.

All her life long Erica remembered that Sunday. The peaceful little church with its high pews, where they sat to sing and stood to pray, the homely German pastor with his plain yet forcible sermon on 'Das Gebet,' the restful feeling of unity which so infinitely outweighed all the trifling differences, and the comfort of the sweet old German chorales. The words of one of them lingered always in her memory.

> 'Fühlt Seel und Leib ein Wohl ergehen
> So treib es mich zum Dank dafür;
> Laszt du mich deine Werke sehen,
> So sey mein Rühmen stets von dir;
> Und find ich in der Welt nicht Ruh,
> So steig mein Sehnen Himmel zu.'

After the service was ended, they wandered out into the public garden where birds were singing round the statue of Walter von der Vogelveide, and a sparrow, to Erica's great delight, perched on his very shoulder. Then they left the town altogether and roamed out into the open country, crossing the river by a long and curiously constructed plank bridge, and sauntering along the valley beneath the snowy mountains, the river flowing smoothly onward, the birds singing, and a paradise of flowers on every side. It was quite the hottest day they had had, and they were not sorry to rest in the first shady place they came to.

'This is the right way to take pleasure,' said

Raeburn, enjoying as only an ardent lover of Nature can enjoy a mountain view. 'Brief snatches in between hard work. More than that is hardly admissible in such times as ours.' His words seemed to them prophetic later on, for their pleasure was destined to be even briefer than they had anticipated. The hotel at which they were staying was being painted. Erica had a room on the second floor, but Raeburn had been put at the top of the house. They had just returned from a long drive, and were quietly sitting in Erica's room writing letters, expecting every moment that the gong would sound for the six o'clock *table-d'hôte*, when a sound of many voices outside made Raeburn look up. He went to the window.

'Hullo! a fire-engine!' he exclaimed.

Erica hastily joined him; a crowd was gathering beneath the window, shouting, waving, gesticulating.

'Why, they are pointing up here!' cried Erica. 'The fire must be here!'

She rushed across the room, and opened the door; the whole place was in an uproar, people rushing to and fro, cries of 'Feuer! Feuer!' a waiter with scared face hurrying from room to room with the announcement, in broken English, 'The hotel is on fire!' or, sometimes, in his haste and confusion, 'The fire is on hotel!' For a moment Erica's heart stood still; the very vagueness of the terror, the uncertainty as to the extent of the danger or the possibility of escape, was paralysing. Then with the natural instinct of a book-lover she hastily picked up two or three volumes from the table, and begged her father to come. He made her put on her hat and cloak, and shouldering her portmanteau, led the way through the corridors and down the staircase, steadily forcing a passage through the confused and terrified people, and never pausing for an instant, not even asking the whereabouts of the fire, till he had got Erica safely out into the little platz, and had set down her portmanteau under one of the trees.

They looked up then and saw that the whole of the roof and the attics of the hotel were blazing. Raeburn's room was immediately below and was in great danger. A sudden thought seemed to occur to him, a look of dismay crossed his face, he felt hurriedly in his pocket.

'Where did I change my coat, Erica?' he asked.

'You went up to your room to change it, just before the drive,' she replied.

'Then, by all that's unlucky I've left in it those papers for Hasenbalg! Wait here; I'll be back in a minute.'

He hurried off, looking more anxious than Erica had ever seen him look before. The papers which he had been asked to deliver to Herr Hasenbalg in no way concerned him, but they had been entrusted to his care, and were therefore, of course, more to be considered than the most valuable private property. Much hindered by the crowd and by the fire-engine itself, which had been moved into the entrance-hall, he at length succeeded in fighting his way past an unceasing procession of furniture which was being rescued from the flames, and pushing his way up the stairs had almost gained his room, when a pitiful cry reached his ears. It was impossible to a man of Raeburn's nature not to turn aside: the political despatches might be very important, but a deserted child in a burning house outweighed all other considerations. He threw open the door of the room whence the cry had come; the scaffolding outside had caught fire and the flames were darting in at the window. Sitting up in a little wooden cot was a child of two or three years old, his baby face wild with fright.

'Poor bairn!' exclaimed Raeburn, taking him in his strong arms. 'Have they forgotten you?'

The child was German and did not understand a word, but it knew in a moment that this man, so like a fairy-tale giant, was a rescuer.

'*Guter Riese!*' it sobbed, appealingly.

The 'good giant' snatched a blanket from the cot, rolled it round the shivering little bit of humanity, and carried him down into the platz.

'Keep this bairnie till his belongings claim him,' he said, putting his charge into Erica's arms. And then he hurried back again, once more ran the gauntlet of the descending wardrobes and bedsteads, and at last reached his room. It was bare of all furniture; the lighter things—his coat among them—had been thrown out of the window, the more solid things had been carried downstairs. He stood there baffled and for once in his life bewildered.

Half-choked with the smoke, he crossed the room and looked out of the window, the hot breath of the flames from the scaffolding scorching his face. But looking through that frame of fire, he saw that a *cordon* had been drawn round the indiscriminate piles of rescued property, that the military had been called out, and that the most perfect order prevailed. There was still a chance that he might recover the lost papers! Then, as there was no knowing that the roof would not fall in and crush him, he made the best of his way down again among the still flowing stream of furniture.

An immense crowd had gathered in the square outside; the awe-struck murmurs and exclamations sounded like the roar of distant thunder, and the shouts of 'Wasser! Wasser!' alternated with the winding of bugles, as the soldiers moved now in one direction, now in another, their bright uniforms and the shining helmets of the fire-brigade men flashing hither and thither among the dark mass of spectators. Overhead the flames raged, while the wind blew down bits of burning tinder upon the crowd. Erica, wedged in among the friendly Tyrolese people, watched anxiously for her father, not quite able to believe his assurance that there was no danger. When at length she saw the tall commanding figure emerge from the burning hotel, the white head towering over the crowd, her heart gave a great bound of relief. But she saw in a moment that he had been unsuccessful.

'It must have been thrown out of the window,' he said, elbowing his way up to her. 'The room was absolutely bare, carpet and all gone, nothing to be found but these valuables,' and with a smile, he held up the last number of the *Idol-Breaker*, and a tooth-brush.

'They are taking great care of the things,' said Erica. 'Perhaps we shall find it by-and-by.'

'We must find it,' said Raeburn, his lips forming into the curve of resoluteness which they were wont to assume when any difficulty arose to be grappled with. 'What has become of the bairn?'

'A nurse came up and claimed it, and was overwhelmingly grateful to you for your rescue. She had put the child to bed early and had gone for a walk in the Gardens. Oh, look, how the fire is spreading!'

'That scaffolding is terribly against saving it, and the wind is high, too,' said Raeburn, scanning the place all over with his keen eyes. Then, as an idea seemed to strike him, he suddenly hurried forward once more, and Erica saw him speaking to two fire-brigade men. In another minute the soldiers motioned the crowd further back, Raeburn rejoined Erica, and, picking up her portmanteau, took her across the road to the steps of a neighbouring hotel. 'I've suggested that they should cut down the scaffolding,' he said; 'it is the only chance of saving the place.'

The whole of the woodwork was now on fire; to cut it down was a somewhat dangerous task, but the men worked gallantly, and in a few minutes the huge blazing frame, with its poles and cross-poles, ladders and platforms, swayed, quivered, then fell forward with a crash into the garden beyond.

Raeburn had, as usual, attracted to himself the person most worth talking to in the crowd, a shrewd-looking inhabitant of Innsbruck, spectacled and somewhat sallow, but with a face which was full of intellect. He learnt that, although no one could speak positively as to the origin of the fire, it was more than probable that it had been no mere accident. The very Sunday before, at exactly the same hour, a large factory had been entirely destroyed by fire, and it needed no very deep thinker to discover that a Sunday evening, when everyone would be out of doors keeping holiday, and the fire-brigade men scattered and hard to summon, was the very time for incendiarism. They learnt much from the shrewd citizen about the general condition of the place, which seemed outwardly too peaceful and prosperous for such wild and senseless outbreaks.

'If, as seems probable, this is the act of some crazy socialist, he has unwittingly done harm to the cause of reform in general,' said Raeburn to Erica, when the informant had passed on. 'Those papers for Hasenbalg were important ones, and, if laid hold of by unfriendly hands, might do untold harm. Socialism is the most foolish system on earth. Inevitably it turns to this sort of violence when the uneducated have seized on its main idea.'

'After all, I believe they will save the house,' said Erica. 'Just look at those men on the top, how splendidly they are working!'

It was, in truth, a grand, though a very horrible sight to see the dark forms toiling away, hewing down the burning rafters with an absolute disregard to their personal safety. These were not firemen, but volunteers—chimney-sweeps, as one of the crowd informed Raeburn —and it was in the main owing to their exertions that the fire was at length extinguished.

After the excitement was over, they went into the neighbouring hotel, where there was some difficulty in obtaining rooms, as all the burnt-out people had taken refuge there. However, the utmost hospitality and friendliness prevailed, and even hungry Englishmen, cheated of their dinner, were patient for once, while the over-taxed waiters hurried to and fro, preparing for the second and quite unexpected *table-d'hôte*. Everyone had something to tell either of his escape or his losses. One lady had seen her nightgown thrown out of the window, and had managed adroitly to catch it; some one else on rushing up to find his purse had been deluged by the fire-engine; and Raeburn's story of the little German boy excited great interest. The visitors were inclined to make a hero of him. Once, when he had left the room, Erica heard a discussion about him with no little amusement.

'Who is the very tall, white-haired man?'

'The one who saved the child? I believe he must be the Bishop of Steneborough; he is travelling in the Tyrol, I know, and I'm sure that man is a somebody. So much dignity and such power over everybody! didn't you see the way the captain of the fire-brigade deferred to him?'

'Well, now I think of it,' replied the other, 'he has an earnest, devotional sort of face; perhaps you're right. I'll speak to him when he comes back. Ah!' in a lower voice, 'there he is! and—confound it! he's got no gaiters! Good-bye to my visions of life-long friendship and a comfortable living for Dick!'

In spite of his anxiety about the lost packet, Raeburn laughed heartily over Erica's account of this conversation. He had obtained leave to search the deserted hotel, and a little before ten o'clock they made their way across the square, over planks and charred rafters, broken glass, and pools of water, which were hard to steer through in the darkness. The fire was now quite out, and they were beginning to move the furniture in again, but the place had been entirely dismantled, and looked eerie and forlorn. On the staircase was a decapitated statue, and broken and crushed plants were strewn about. Erica's room was perfectly bare of furniture, nor could she find any of the things she wanted. The pen with which she had been writing lay on the floor, and also a Japanese fan soaked with water, but neither of these were very serviceable articles to a person bereft of every toilete requisite.

'I shall have to lie down to-night like a dog, and get up in the morning, and shake myself,' she said, laughing.

And probably a good many people in Innsbruck were that evening in like case.

Notwithstanding the discomforts, however, and the past excitement, that was the first night in which Erica had really slept since the day at Fiesole, the first night unbroken by dreams about Brian, unhaunted by that blanched, rigid face, which had stamped its image indelibly upon her brain in the amphitheatre. She awoke, too, without that almost intolerable dread of the coming day which had hitherto made early morning hateful to her. It was everything to have an actual and practicable duty ready to hand, everything to have a busy present which would crowd out past and future, if only for a few hours. Also the disaster had its comic side. Through the thin partition she could hear distinctly the complaints of the people in the next room.

'How *are* we to get on with no soap? Do go and see if James has any.'

Then came steps in the passage, and a loud knock at the opposite door.

'James!'

No answer. A furiously loud second knock.

'*James!*'

'What's the matter? Another fire?'

'Have you any soap?'

'Any what?' sleepily.

'Any *soap?*'

Apparently James was not the happy possessor of that necessary of life, for the steps retreated, and the bell was violently rung.

'"What, no soap!"' exclaimed Erica, laughing; '"so he died, and she very imprudently married the barber, etc."'

The chambermaid came to answer the bell.

'Send some one to the nearest shop, please, and get me some soap.'

'And a sponge,' said another.

'And a brush and comb,' said the first.

'Oh! and some hair-pins,' echoed the other. 'Why, distraction! she doesn't understand a word! What's the German for soap? Give me "Travel Talk."'

'It's burnt.'

'Well, then, show her the soap-dish! Brush your hair with your hands! This is something between Dumb Crambo and Mulberry Bush!'

The whole day was not unlike a fatiguing game of hide-and-seek, and had it not been for Raeburn's great anxiety, it would have been exceedingly amusing. Everything was now inside the hotel again, but of course in the wildest confusion. The personal property of the visitors was placed, as it came to light, in the hall-porter's little room; but things were to be met with in all directions. At ten o'clock, one of Raeburn's boots was found on the third storey; in the evening, its fellow turned up in the entrance-hall. Distracted tourists were to be seen in all directions, burrowing under heaps of clothes, or vainly opening cupboards and drawers, and the delight of finding even the most trifling possession was great. For hours Raeburn and Erica searched for the lost papers in vain. At length, in the evening, the coat was found; but, alas! the pocket was empty.

'The envelope must have been taken out,' said Erica. 'Was it directed?'

'Unfortunately, yes,' said Raeburn. 'But, after all, there is still a chance that it may have tumbled out as the coat fell. If so, we may find it elsewhere. I've great faith in the honesty of these Innsbruck people, notwithstanding the craze of some of them that property is theft.

That worthy man yesterday was right, I expect. I hear that the proprietor had had a threatening letter not long ago to this effect—

> " Sein thun unser Dreiszig,
> Schüren thun wir fleiszig,
> Dem Armen thät's nichts,
> Dem Reichen schad'ts nichts."

That is tolerably unmistakable, I think. I'll have it in next week's *Idol*, with an article on the folly of Socialism.'

Judicious offers of reward failed to bring the papers to light, and Raeburn was so much vexed about it, and so determined to search every nook and cranny of the hotel, that it was hard to get him away even for meals. Erica could not help feeling that it was hard that the brief days of relaxation he had allowed himself should be so entirely spoilt.

'Now, if I were a model daughter, I should dream where to find the thing,' she said, laughingly, as she wished him good-night.

She did not dream at all, but she was up as soon as it was light, searching once more with minute faithfulness in every part of the hotel. At length she came to a room piled from floor to ceiling with linen, blankets, and coverlets.

'Have all these been shaken?' she asked of the maid-servant who had been helping her.

'Well, not shaken, I think,' owned the servant. 'We were in a hurry, you see; but they are all fresh folded.'

'It might have slipped into one of them,' said Erica. 'Help me to shake every one of these, and I will give you two gulden.'

It was hard work, and somewhat hopeless work; but Erica set about it with all the earnestness and thoroughness of her Raeburn nature, and at length came her reward. At the very bottom of the huge pile they came to a counterpane, and, as they opened it, out fell the large, thick envelope directed to Herr Hasenbalg. With a cry of joy, Erica snatched it up, pressed double the reward into the hands of the delighted servant, and flew in search of her father. She found him groping in a great heap of miscellaneous goods in the porter's room.

'I've found my razors,' he said, looking up, 'and every twopenny-halfpenny thing out of my travelling-bag; but the papers, of course, are nowhere.'

'What's your definition of "nowhere"?' asked Erica, laughingly covering his eyes, while she slipped the envelope into his hand.

His look of relief made her happier than she had been for days. He stood up quickly, and turned the envelope over to see that it had not been tampered with.

'This is my definition of a dear, good bairn,' he said, putting his hand on her head. 'You have taken a hundredweight off my heart, Eric. Where did you find it?'

She described her search to him.

'Well, now, nothing will satisfy me but a mountain,' said Raeburn. 'Are you too tired? We could have a good climb before dinner.'

'Oh, let us!' she exclaimed. 'I have had such a longing to get nearer the snow.'

Each felt that the holiday had now begun. They threw care to the winds, and gave themselves up altogether to the enjoyment of the loveliest walk they had ever taken. Crossing the Kreuzer bridge, they made their way past little wooden châlets, through groves of oak.

where the sunlight came flickering in between the leaves, through pine-woods whose long vistas were solemn as cathedral aisles, until at last they gained the summit of the lower range of hills, from which was a glorious view on every hand. Down below lay the little town which would be for ever memorable to them; while above them rose the grand chain of snowy mountains which still seemed as lofty and unapproachable as ever, though they themselves were on high ground. Soft and velvety and green lay that great upward sweep in the sunshine, shaded in some places by a dark patch of pines, or gleaming with a heap of fallen snow. Here and there some deep rugged cleft would be filled from top to bottom with the gleaming whiteness, while above, crowning the steep and barren height, the snow reigned supreme, unmelted as yet even by the hot May sun.

And Erica was, in spite of her sorrow, unfeignedly happy. She could not be sad when her father was so thoroughly enjoying himself, when for once he was altogether removed from the baleful influences of hatred, malice, and all uncharitableness. Here—instead of sweeping denunciations, which invariably drove him, as they drove even the patient Job, to an assertion of his own righteousness—there was the silent yet most real teaching of Nature; and he must be a small-souled man, indeed, who, in the presence of grand mountain scenery, cannot forget his own personality, realising the infinite beauty and the unspeakable greatness of Nature. Erica's father was unquestionably a large-souled man, in every sense of the word a great man; but the best man in the world is to a great extent dependent on circumstance, and the circumstances of Raeburn's life had been exceptionally hard. Only two things on earth acted as a check upon the one great fault which marred an otherwise fine character. Beauty of scenery made him for the time being as humble as a child, and the devotion of his own followers sometimes made him ask himself whether he were worthy of such love.

The following day the papers, which had caused them so much trouble and anxiety, were safely delivered to Herr Hasenbalg at Salzburg;

and then came one more perfect holiday. In the months that followed Erica loved just to shut her eyes and forget a sad or stormy present, to call up once more the remembrance of that time. To the minutest details she always remembered it. The start in the early morning, which had seemed cloudy and unpromising, the long, beautiful drive to Berchtesgaden, and on beyond to the Königsee. The perfect and unbroken calm of that loveliest of lakes, so jealously guarded by its chain of mountains that only in two places is it possible to effect a landing. The dark pines and silvery birches clothing the sides of the mountains; the grey limestone cliffs rising steep and sheer from the water, in which their slim, green skiff glided swiftly on, the oars, which were more like long, brown spades, pulled by a man and woman, who took it in turns to sit and stand: the man with gay tie and waistband, Tyrolese hat and waving feather; the woman wearing a similar hat over a gaily-embroidered head-dress, ample white sleeves, a square-cut bodice, and blue plaid skirt.

Here and there a group of light-green larches

just caught the sunshine, or a little boat coming in the opposite direction would suddenly glide round one of the bends in the lake, its oars splashing a wide line of silvery brightness in the calm water, in vivid contrast to the dark-blue prow. Then, as they rounded one of the abrupt curves, came a glorious view of snow-mountains—blue shadows below, and above, in the sunshine, the most dazzling whiteness, while close to the water, from the sheer precipice of grey rock, sprang here and there a hardy pine.

They landed beside a quaint little church with cupolas, and had an exquisite walk through the woods just at the foot of the mountains, where the wealth of gentians and other Alpine flowers made Raeburn's felicity complete.

Presently came the return to the little boat, and a quiet row back to the landing-place, where their carriage awaited them. And then followed the delightful drive home, past the river, which tossed its green waters here and there into snow-like wreaths of foam, over quaint and shaky wooden bridges, between grey rocks and groves of plane-trees, whose trunks were half veiled in golden-brown moss. Then on beneath a hill covered with young pines, which grew to the very road-side, catching far-away glimpses of a darkened and mysterious sky through the forest of stems. Then past larger and taller pine-trees, which, standing further apart, let in more sky, and left space for the brown earth to be flecked with sunshine. And here, in the most peaceful of all country regions, they met a handsome-looking peasant, in gay Tyrolese attire, much adorned with silver chains, since it was Ascension Day and a festival. He was leading by the hand his little daughter.

'That is a peaceful lot,' said Raeburn, glancing at them. 'Would we like to change places with them, little son Eric?'

She laughed and shook her head, but fell, nevertheless, into a reverie, wondering what such a character as her father's would have been under less hard circumstances, trying to picture a possible life in that sheltered green valley. All was so perfectly peaceful; the very river grew broader and calmer, cattle grazed by the roadside, women walked slowly along with their knitting in their hands, the fruit-trees were white with blossom. As they reached the pretty village of Berchtesgaden the sun was setting, the square, comfortable-looking white houses, with their broad dark eaves and balconies, were bathed in a rosy glow, the two spires of the little church stood out darkly against the evening sky; in the platz women were filling their pitchers at a stone fountain made in the shape of a rampant lion, while others were kneeling before the calvary at the entrance to the village, praying with the reverence which is one of the characteristics of the Tyrolese. Towering above all in the background rose the two Wartzmann peaks, standing there white and majestic like guardian angels.

'What foolish being called seven the perfect number?' said Raeburn, turning back from a last look at the twin mountains which were now assuming their cloud caps. 'Two is the perfect number, is it not, little one?'

She smiled and slipped her hand into his.

Then came a wild, desolate part of the road, which passed through a valley shut-in on all sides by mountains, some of them snowy, all wild and precipitous, and looking strangely desolate in the failing light. Erica could not help contrasting it with the view from the amphitheatre at Fiesole, of that wider amphitheatre of green hills all glowing with light and love. But presently came more peaceful glimpses; pretty little Schellenburg with its serpentine river winding again and again through the village street, and the happy-looking peasants chatting at their doors with here and there a white-capped baby made much of by all.

At last in the cool of the evening they reached Salzburg once more. But the pleasures of the day were not yet over, for as they drew up at the door of their hotel a well-known figure suddenly emerged from the porch and hurried towards the carriage.

'Unexpected as a meteor,' said a hearty voice, in slightly foreign accents. 'Well, my good friend, well, my guardian angel, how are you both? We meet under more auspicious circumstances this time!'

It was Eric Haeberlein.

## CHAPTER IV.

### THE MOST UNKINDEST CUT OF ALL.

Those who persecuted them supposed of course that they were defending Christianity, but Christianity can be defended in no such way. It forbids all persecution—all prosecution for the sake of religion. Force cannot possibly propagate the truth or produce the faith, or promote the love in which the gospel consists. . . . Persecution can never arise from the zeal for the Gospel as truth—from zeal for the Gospel properly understood. If ever due to zeal in any measure, and not to pride, selfishness, anger, ambition, and other hateful lusts . . . it must be to a zeal which is in alliance with error . . . The men [atheists] therefore, who, by their courage and endurance were specially instrumental in convincing their countrymen that persecution for the avowal and advocacy even of atheism is a folly and a crime, have really rendered a service to the cause of Christian truth, and their names will not be recorded without honour when the history of our century is impartially written.
*Baird Lectures*, 1877.
R. FLINT, D.D., Professor of Divinity, Edinburgh.

A FEW days later the brief holiday ended, and father and daughter were both hard at work again in London. They had crossed from Antwerp by night, and had reached home about ten o'clock, to find the usual busy life awaiting them.

Tom and Aunt Jean, who had been very dull in their absence, were delighted to have them back again; and though the air was thick with coming troubles, yet it was nevertheless a real homecoming, while Erica, in spite of her hidden sorrow, had a very real enjoyment in describing her first foreign tour. They were making a late breakfast while she talked, Raeburn being more or less absorbed in the *Daily Review.*

'You see such an early newspaper is a luxury now,' said Erica. 'Not that he's been behaving well abroad. He promised me when we started that he'd eschew newspapers altogether, and give his brain an entire rest; but there is a beguiling reading-room at Florence, and there was no keeping him away from it.

'What's that? What are you saying?' said Raeburn, absently.

'That very soon, father, you will be as absent-minded as King Stars-and-Garters in the fairy tale, who one day, in a fit of abstraction, buttered his newspaper, and tried to read his toast.'

Raeburn laughed, and threw down the *Daily Review*.

'Saucier than ever, isn't she, Tom? Well, we've come back to a few disagreeables; but then we've come back, thank—man! to roast beef and Turkey towels, and after kickshaws and table-napkins, one knows how to appreciate such things.'

'We could have done with your kickshaws here,' said Tom. 'If you hadn't come back soon, Erica, I should have gone to the bad altogether; for home-life, with the cook to cater for one, is intolerable. That creature has only two ideas in her head! We rang the changes on rice and stewed rhubarb. The rhubarb in its oldest stage came up four days running. We called it the widow's cruse! Then the servants would make a point of eating onions for supper, so that the house was insufferable. And at last we were driven from pillar to post by a dreadful process called house-cleaning, in which, undoubtedly, life is not worth living. In the end, Mr. Osmond took pity on me, and lent me Brian's study. Imagine heretical writings emanating from that room!'

This led the conversation round to Brian's visit to Florence, and Erica was not sorry to be interrupted by a note from Mr. Bircham, requesting her to write an article on the Kilbeggan murder. She found that the wheels of the household machinery would need a good deal of attention before they would move as smoothly as she generally contrived to make them. Things had somehow 'got to wrongs' in her absence. And when at length she thought everything was in train, and had got thoroughly into the spirit of a descriptive article on the Irish tragedy, the cook of two ideas interrupted her with what seemed, in contrast, the most trivial of matters.

'If you please, miss,' she said, coming into the green-room just as the three villains in black masks were in the act of killing their victim, 'I thought you'd wish to know that we are wanting a new set of kitchen-cloths; and if you'll excuse me mentioning it, miss, there's Jane, miss, using glass-cloths as tea-cloths, and dusters as knife-cloths.'

Erica looked slightly distracted, but diverted her mind from the state of Ireland to the state of the household linen, and, when left alone once more, laughed to herself at the incongruity of the two subjects.

It was nearly a fortnight before Brian returned from Switzerland. Erica knew that he was in the well-known house on the opposite side of the square, and through the trees in the garden they could each see the other's place of residence. It was a sort of nineteenth century version of the Rhine legend, in which the knight of Rolandseck looked down upon Nonnenwerth, where his lady-love was immured in a convent.

She had rather dreaded the first meeting, but, when it came, she felt nothing of what she had feared. She was in the habit of going on Sunday morning to the eight o'clock service at the church in the square. It was nearer than Charles Osmond's church, and the hour interfered less with household arrangements. Just at the corner of the square, on the morning of Trinity Sunday, she met Brian. Her heart beat quickly as she shook hands with him, but there was something in his bearing which set her entirely at her ease after just the first minute. He looked much older, and a certain restlessness in look and manner had quite left him, giving place to a peculiar calm not unlike his father's expression. It was the expression which a man bears when he has lost the desire of his heart, yet manfully struggles on, allowing no bitterness to steal in, facing unflinchingly the greyness of a crippled life. Somehow, joining in that thanksgiving service seemed to give them the true key-note for their divided lives. As they came out into the porch, he asked her a question.

'You are an authority on quotations, I know; my father wants to verify one for his sermon this morning. Can you help him? it is this:

> " Revealed in love and sacrifice,
> The Holiest passed before thine eyes,
> One and the same, in threefold guise." '

'It is Whittier, I know,' said Erica, promptly; and I think it is in a poem called "Trinitas." Come home with me, and we will hunt for it.'

So they walked back together silently, and found the poem, and at Raeburn's request Brian stayed to breakfast, and fell back naturally into his old place with them all.

The following day Raeburn had to attend a meeting in the north of England; he returned on the Tuesday afternoon, looking, Erica fancied, tired and overdone.

'Railway journeys are not quite the rest they once were to me,' he confessed, throwing himself down in a chair by the open window, while she brought him some tea. 'This is very beguiling, little one; but see, I've all these letters to answer before five.'

'Your train must have been very late.'

'Yes, there was a block on the line, and we stopped for half-an-hour in the middle of a bean-field—bliss that a Londoner can't often enjoy.'

'Did you get out?'

'Oh, yes, and sat upon the fence and meditated, to the great delectation of my olfactory nerves.'

Erica's laugh was checked by a knock at the

door. The servant announced that a gentleman wanted to see Miss Raeburn.

'Some message from Mr. Bircham, I expect,' said Erica to her father. 'Ask him upstairs, please. I only hope he doesn't want me to write another article at the eleventh hour. If it's the little Irish sub-editor, you must be very polite to him, father, for he has been kind to me.'

But it was no message from the *Daily Review* office; a perfect stranger was shown into the room.

He bowed slightly as he entered.

'Are you Miss Erica Raeburn?' he asked, coming towards her.

'I am,' she replied. 'What is your business with me?'

'I have to place this document in your hands.'

He gave her a paper, which she rapidly unfolded. To her dying day she could always see that hateful bit of foolscap, with its alternate printing and writing. The words were to this effect:

WRIT SUBPŒNA AD TEST, AT SITTINGS OF HIGH COURT.

### In the High Court of Justice, Queen's Bench Division.

Between LUKE RAEBURN, Plaintiff,

AND

WILLIAM HENRY POGSON, Defendant.

VICTORIA, by the Grace of God, of the United Kingdom of Great Britain and Ireland, Queen, Defender of the Faith,

To ERICA RAEBURN, greeting.

We command you to attend at the sittings of the QUEEN'S BENCH DIVISION of our HIGH COURT OF JUSTICE to be holden at WESTMINSTER, on Tuesday the Twentieth day of June, 18—, at the hour of half-past Ten in the forenoon, and so from day to day during the said sittings, until the above cause is tried, to give evidence on behalf of the Defendant.

Witness, etc., etc.

Erica read the paper twice before she looked up; she had grown white to the very lips. Raeburn, recognising the form of a subpœna, came hastily forward, and in the merest glance saw how matters were. By no possibility could the most malicious of opponents have selected a surer means of torturing him.

'Is this legal?' asked Erica, lifting to his eyes that flashed with righteous indignation.

'Oh, it is legal,' he replied, bitterly—'the pound of flesh was legal. A wife need not appear against her husband, but a daughter may be dragged into court and forced to give evidence against her father.'

As he spoke, such anger flashed from his eyes that the clerk shivered all down his backbone. He thought he would take his departure as quickly as might be, and drawing a little nearer, put down a coin upon the table beside Erica.

'This fee is to cover your expenses, madam,' he said.

'What!' exclaimed Erica, her anger leaping up into a sudden flame, 'do you think I shall take money from that man?'

She had an insane desire to snatch up the sovereign and fling it at the clerk's head, but, restraining herself, merely flicked it back across the table to him, just touching it with the back of her hand, as though it had been polluted.

'You can take that back again,' she said, a look of scorn sweeping over her face. 'Tell Mr. Pogson that, when he martyrs people, he need not say, "The martyrdom will make you hungry—here is luncheon money," or "The torture will tire you—here is your cab-fare!"'

'But, madam, excuse me,' said the clerk looking much embarrassed, 'I must leave the money, I am bound to leave it.'

'If you leave it, I shall just throw it into the fire-place before your eyes,' said Erica. 'But if indeed it can't be sent back, then give it to the first gutter-child you meet—do anything you like with it! hang it on your watch-chain as a memento of the most cruel case your firm ever had to do with!'

Her colour had come back again, her cheeks were glowing, in her wrath she looked most beautiful; the clerk would have been less than human if he had not felt sorry for her. There was a moment's silence; he glanced from the daughter to the father whose face was still pale and rigid. A great pity surged up in the clerk's heart. He was a father himself, involuntarily his thoughts turned to the little home at Kilburn where Mary and Kitty would be waiting for him that evening. What if they should ever be forced into a witness-box to confirm a libel on his personal character? A sort of moisture came to his eyes at the bare idea. The counsel for the defence, too, was that Cringer, Q.C. the greatest bully that ever wore silk! Then he glanced once more at the silent majestic figure with the rigid face, who though an atheist was yet a man and a father.

'Sir,' he said, with the ring of real and deep feeling in his voice, 'sir, believe me, if I had known what bringing this subpœna meant, I would sooner have lost my situation!'

Raeburn's face relaxed; he spoke a few courteous, dignified words, accepting with a sort of unspoken gratitude the man's regret, and in a few moments dismissing him. But, even in those few moments the clerk, though by no means an impressionable man, had felt the spell, the strange power of fascination which Raeburn invariably exercised upon those he talked with—that inexplicable influence which made cautious, hard-headed mechanics ready to die for him, ready to risk anything in his cause.

The instant the man was gone, Raeburn sat down at Erica's writing-table and began to answer his letters. His correspondents got very curt answers that day. Erica could tell by the sound of his pen how sharp were the down-strokes, how short the rapidly written sentences.

'Can I help you?' she asked, drawing nearer to him.

He hastily selected two or three letters not bearing on his anti-religious work, gave her directions, then plunged his pen in the ink once more, and went on writing at lightning speed. When at length the most necessary ones were done, he pushed back his chair, and getting up began to pace rapidly to and fro. Presently he paused, and leaned against the mantelpiece, his face half shaded by his hand.

Erica stole up to him silently.

'Sometimes, Eric,' he said, abruptly, 'I feel the need of the word " *Devil*." My vocabulary has nothing strong enough for that man.'

She was too heartsick to speak; she drew closer to him with a mute caress.

'Eric!' he said, holding her hands between his, and looking down at her with an indescribably eager expression in his eyes, 'Eric, surely *now* you see that this persecuting religion, this religion which has been persecuting innumerable people for hundreds of years, is false, worthless, rotten to the core! Child! child! surely you can't believe in a God whose followers try to promote His glory by sheer brutality like this?'

It was the first time he had spoken to her on this subject since their interview at Codrington. They had resolved never to touch upon it again; but a sort of consciousness that some good must come to him through this new bitterness, a hope that it must and would reconvince his child, impelled Raeburn to break his resolution.

'I could sooner doubt that you are standing here, father, with your arm round me,' said Erica, 'than I could doubt the presence of your Father and mine—the All-Father.'

'Even though His followers are such lying scoundrels as that Pogson? What do you make of that? What do you think of that?'

'I think,' she replied, quietly, 'that my father is too just a man to judge Christianity by the very worst specimen of a Christian to be met with. Anyone who does not judge Secularism by its very best representatives, dead or living, is unfair—and what is unfair in one case is unfair in another.'

'Well, if I judged it by you, perhaps I might take a different view of it,' said Raeburn. 'But then you had the advantage of some years of Secularism.'

'Not by me!' cried Erica. 'How can it seem anything but very faulty when you judge it only by faulty people? Why not judge it by the life and character of Christ?'

Raeburn turned away with a gesture of impatience.

'A myth! a poetic creation—long ago distorted out of its true proportions! There, child, I see we must stop. I only pain you and torture myself by arguing the question.'

'One more thing,' said Erica, 'before we go back to the old silence. Father, if you would only write a life of Christ—I mean, a really complete life; the one you wrote years ago was scarcely more than a pamphlet.'

He smiled a little, knowing that she thought the deep study necessary for such an undertaking would lead to a change in his views.

'My dear,' he said, 'perhaps I would; but just see how I am overdone. I couldn't write an elaborate thing now. Besides, there is the book on the Pentateuch not half finished, though it was promised months ago. Perhaps a year or two hence, when Pogson gives me time to draw a long breath, I'll attempt it; but I have an idea that one or other of us will have to be "kilt intirely" before that happy time arrives. Perhaps we shall mutually do for each other, and re-enact the historical song.' And, with laughter in his eyes, he repeated,

'There once were two cats of Kilkenny,
Each thought there was one cat too many,
So they quarrelled and spit, and they scratched and they bit,
Till, excepting their nails and the tips of their tails,
Instead of two cats, there weren't any.'

Erica smiled faintly, but sighed the next minute.

'Well, there! it's too grave a matter to jest about,' said Raeburn. 'Oh, bairn! if I could but save you from that brute's malice, I should care very little for the rest.'

'Since you only care about it for my sake, and I only for yours, I think we may as well give up caring at all,' said Erica, looking up at him with a brave smile. 'And, after all, Mr. Cringer, Q.C., can only keep me in purgatory for a few hours at the outside. Don't you think, too, that such a cruel thing will damage Mr. Pogson in the eyes of the jury?'

'Unfortunately, dear, juries are seldom inclined to show any delicate considerateness to an atheist,' said Raeburn.

And Erica knew that he spoke truly enough.

No more was said just then. Raeburn began rapidly to run through his remaining correspondence—a truly miscellaneous collection. Legal letters, political letters, business letters,—requests for his autograph, for his help, for his advice;—a challenge from a Presbyterian minister in the north of Scotland to meet him in debate; the like from a Unitarian in Norfolk; a coffin and some insulting verses in a match-box, and lastly an abusive letter from a clergyman, holding him responsible for some articles by Mr. Masterman, which he had nothing whatever to do with, and of which he in fact disapproved.

'What would they think, Eric, if I insisted on holding the Bishop of London responsible for every utterance of every Christian in the diocese?' said Raeburn.

'They would think you were a fool,' said Erica, cutting the coffin into little bits as she spoke.

Raeburn smiled and pencilled a word or two on the letter—the pith of a stinging reply.

## CHAPTER V.

### RAEBURN *v.* POGSON.

Oh, God of mountains, stars, and boundless spaces!
Oh, God of freedom and of joyous hearts!
When Thy face looketh forth from all men's faces,
There will be room enough in crowded marts.
Brood Thou around me, and the noise is o'er;
Thy universe my closet with shut door.

Heart, heart, awake! The love that loveth all
Maketh a deeper calm than Horeb's cave.
God in thee, can His children's folly gall?
Love may be hurt, but shall not love be brave?
Thy holy silence sinks in dews of balm;
Thou art my solitude, my mountain calm.
GEORGE MAC DONALD.

WHEN a particularly unpleasant event has long been hanging over one's head, sure to come at some time, though the precise date is unknown, people of a certain disposition find it perfectly possible to live on pretty comfortably through

VOL. III. I

the waiting time. But when at length the date is fixed, when you know that that which you dread will happen upon such and such a day, then the waiting begins all at once to seem intolerable. The vague date had been awaited calmly, but the certain date is awaited with a wearing anxiety which tells fearfully on physical strength. When Erica knew that the action for libel would begin in a fortnight's time, the comparative calmness of the nine months which had passed since the outset of the matter gave place to a perfect agony of apprehension. Night after night she had fearful dreams of being cross-examined by Mr. Cringer, Q.C., who always forced her to say exactly what she did not mean. Night after night coldly curious eyes stared down at her from all parts of a crowded court; while her misery was completed by being perfectly conscious of what she ought to have said directly it was too late.

By day she was too wise to allow herself to dwell on the future; she worked doubly hard, laid-in a stock of particularly interesting books, and threw herself as much as possible into the lives of others. Happily, the Farrants were in town, and she was able to see a great deal of them; while on the very day before the trial came a substantial little bit of happiness.

She was sitting in the study doing some copying for her father, when a brougham stopped at the door. Erica, who never failed to recognise a horse if she had once seen it before, who even had favourites among the dozens of omnibus horses which she met daily in Oxford Street, at once knew that either Donovan or Gladys had come to see her.

She ran out into the hall to meet them, but had no sooner opened the study door, than the tiniest of dogs trotted into the room, and began sniffing cautiously at her father's clothes.

'Tottie has made a very unceremonious entrance,' said a clear, mellow voice in the passage. 'May we come in, or are you too busy to-day?'

'Oh, please come in. Father is at home, and I do so want you to meet,' said Erica. 'You have brought Dolly, too, that is delightful. We are dreadfully in want of something young and happy to cheer us up.'

The two men shook hands, with the momentary keen glance into each other's eyes which those give who have heard much of one another but have never been personally acquainted.

'As to Dolly,' said Donovan, 'she requires no introduction to Mr. Raeburn.'

'No,' said Erica, laughing, 'she cried all over his coat two years ago '

Dolly did not often wait for introductions, unless she disliked people. And no child could have found it in its heart to dislike anything so big and kind and fatherly as Luke Raeburn.

'We blought a little dog for Elica,' she said, in her silvery treble.

And the next moment she was established on Raeburn's knee, encouraged to thrust a little, dimpled hand into his pocket for certain Edinburgh dainties.

'Dolly does not beat about the bush,' said Donovan, smiling. 'Would you at all care to have this small animal? I knew you were fond of dogs, and Gladys and I saw this little toy Esquimaux the other day, and fell in love with him. I find, though, that another dog rather hurts Wair's feelings, so you will be doing a kindness to him as well, if you will accept Tottie.'

'Oh, how delightful of you! it was kind of you to think of it,' said Erica. 'I have always so longed to have a dog of my own. And this is such a little beauty! Is it not a very rare breed?'

'I believe it is, and I think he's a loving little beggar, too,' replied Donovan. 'He is making himself quite at home here, is he not?'

And in truth the small dog seemed deeply interested in his new residence. He was the tiniest of his kind, and was covered with long black hair which stood straight up on end; his pointed nose, bright brown eyes, and cunning little ears, set in the framework of bushy hair, gave him a most sagacious appearance. And just now he was brimful of curiosity, pattering all over the room, poking his nose into a great pile of *Idol-Breakers,* sniffing at theological and anti-theological books with perfect impartiality, rubbing himself against Raeburn's foot in the most ingratiating way, and finally springing up on Erica's lap with the oddest mixture of defiance and devotion in his eyes, which said as plainly as if he had spoken, 'People may say what they like about you, but I'm your faithful dog from this day forward!'

Raeburn was obliged to go out almost directly, as he had an appointment in the city, but Erica knew that he had seen enough of Donovan to realise what he was, and was satisfied.

'I am so glad you have just met,' she said, when he had left the room. 'And, as to Dolly, she's been a real god-send. I haven't seen my father smile before for a week.'

'Strange, is it not, how almost always children instinctively take to those whom the world treats as outcasts! I have a great belief that God lets the pure and innocent make up in part by their love for the uncharitableness of the rest of us.'

'That's a nice thought,' said Erica. 'I have never had much to do with children, except with this one.' And as she spoke she lifted Dolly on her lap beside Tottie.

'I have good reason to believe in both this kind and that,' said Donovan, touching the dusky head of the dog and the sunny hair of the child. As he spoke, there was a look in his eyes which made Erica feel inclined almost to cry. She knew that he was thinking of the past, though there was no regret in his expression, only a shade of additional gravity about his lips, and an unusual light about his brow and eyes. It was the face of a man who had known both the evil and the good, and had now reached far into the Unseen.

By-and-by they talked of Switzerland, and of Brian, Donovan telling her just what she wanted to know about him, though he never let her feel that he knew all about the day at Fiesole. And from that they passed to the coming trial, of which he spoke in exactly the most helpful way, not trying to assure her, as some well-meaning people had done, that there was really nothing to be grieved or anxious about; but fully sympathising with the pain, while he somehow led her on to the thought of the unseen good which would in the long-run result from it.

'I do believe that now, with all my heart,' she said.

'I knew you did,' he replied, smiling a little. 'You have learnt it since you were at Greyshot last year. And once learnt, it is learnt for ever.'

'Yes,' she said, musingly. 'But, oh! how

slowly one learns in such little bits! It's a great mistake to think that we grasp the whole when the light first comes to us; and yet it feels then like the whole.'

'Because it was the whole you were then capable of,' said Donovan. ' But, you see, you grow.'

'Want to grow, at any rate,' said Erica. 'Grow conscious that there is an Infinite to grow to.'

Then, as in a few minutes he rose to go,

'Well! you have done me good, you and Dolly, and this blessed little dog. Thank you very much for coming.'

She went out with them to the door, and stood on the steps, with Tottie in her arms, smiling a good-bye to little Dolly.

'That's the bravest woman I know,' thought Donovan to himself, 'and the sweetest—save one. Poor Brian! Though, after all, it's a grand thing to love such as Erica even without hope.'

And all the afternoon there rang in his ears the line—

'A woman's soul, most soft yet strong.'

The next day troubles began in good earnest. They were all very silent at breakfast; Raeburn looked anxious and pre-occupied, and Erica, not feeling sure that conversation would not worry him, did not try to talk. Once Aunt Jean looked up for a moment from her paper with a question.

'By-the-by, what are you going to wear, Erica?'

'Sackcloth, I think,' said Erica; 'it would be appropriate.'

Raeburn smiled a little at this.

'Something cool, I should advise,' he said. 'The place will be like a furnace to-day.'

He pushed back his chair as he spoke, and went away to his study. Tom had to hurry away, too, being due at his office by nine o'clock; and Erica began to rack her brains to devise the nicest of dinners for them that evening. She dressed in good time, and was waiting for her father in the green-room, when just before ten o'clock the front door opened, quick steps came up the stairs, and, to her amazement, Tom entered.

'Back again!' she exclaimed. 'Have you got a holiday?'

'I've got my *congé*,' he said, in a hoarse voice, throwing himself down in a chair by the window.

'Tom! What do you mean?' she cried, dismayed by the trouble in his face.

'Got the sack,' he said, shortly.

'What! Lost your situation? But how? Why?'

'I was called this morning into Mr. Ashgrove's private room; he informed me that he had just learnt with great annoyance that I was the nephew of that (you can supply his string of abusive adjectives) Luke Raeburn. Was it true? I told him I had that honour. Was I, then, an atheist? Certainly. A Raeburnite? Naturally. After which came a long jobation, at the end of which I found myself the wrong side of the office door, with orders never to darken it again, and next month's salary in my hand. That's the matter in brief, *Cugina*.'

His face settled into a sort of blank despair,

so unlike its usual expression that Erica's wrath flamed up at the sight.

'It's a shame!' she cried—'a wicked shame! Oh, Tom dear, I am so sorry for you. I wish this had come upon me instead.'

'I wouldn't care so much,' said poor Tom, huskily, 'if he hadn't chosen just this time for it; but it will worry the chieftain now.'

Erica was on the verge of tears.

'Oh, what shall we do—what can we do?' she cried, almost in despair. 'I had not thought of that. Father will feel it dreadfully.'

But to conceal the matter was now hopeless, for as she spoke Raeburn came into the room.

'What shall I feel dreadfully?' he said, smiling a little. 'If any man ought to be case-hardened, I ought to be.'

But as he drew nearer, and saw the faces of the two, his own face grew stern and anxious.

'You at home, Tom! What's the matter?'

Tom briefly told his tale, trying to make as light of it as possible, even trying to force a little humour into his account, but with poor success. There was absolute silence in the green-room when he paused. Raeburn said not a word, but he grew very pale, evidently in this matter being by no means case-hardened. A similar instance, further removed from his immediate circle, might have called forth a strong, angry denunciation; but he felt too deeply anything affecting his own family or friends to be able in the first keenness of his grief and anger to speak.

'My boy,' he said at last, in the low, musical voice whose perfect modulations taxed Tom's powers of endurance to the utmost, 'I am very sorry for this. I can't say more now; we will talk it over to-night. Will you come to Westminster with us?'

And presently, as they drove along the crowded streets, he said, with a bitter smile,

'There's one Biblical woe which by no possibility can ever befall us.'

'What's that?' said Tom.

'"Woe unto you when all men speak well of you,"' said Raeburn.

A few minutes later, and the memorable trial of Raeburn *v.* Pogson had at length begun.

Raeburn's friends had done their best to dissuade him from conducting his own case, but he always replied to them with one of his Scotch proverbs, 'A man's a lion in his ain cause.' His opening speech was such an exceedingly powerful one that all felt on the first day that he had been right, though inevitably it added not a little to the disagreeableness of the case.

As soon as the court had risen, Erica went home with her aunt and Tom, thankful to feel that at least one day was well over; but her father was closeted for some hours with his solicitor, and did not rejoin them till late that evening. He came in then, looking fearfully tired, and scarcely spoke all through dinner; but afterwards, just as Tom was leaving the room, he called him back.

'I've been thinking things over,' he said. 'What was your salary with Mr. Ashgrove?'

'£100 a year,' replied Tom, wondering at what possible hour the chieftain had found a spare moment to bestow upon his affairs.

'Well, then, will you be my secretary for the same?'

For many years Tom had given all his spare time to helping Raeburn with his correspondence, and for some time he had been the practical, though unrecognised, sub-editor of the *Idol-Breaker;* but all his work had been done out of pure devotion to the 'cause.' Nothing could have pleased him more than to give his whole time to the work, while his great love and admiration for Raeburn eminently qualified him for the service of a somewhat autocratic master.

Raeburn, with all his readiness to help those in any difficulty, with all his geniality and thoroughness of character, was by no means the easiest person to work with. For, in common with other strong and self-reliant characters, he liked in all things to have his own way, and being in truth a first-rate organiser, he had scant patience with other people's schemes. Erica was very glad that he had made the proposal to Tom, for, though regretting that he should give his life to the furtherance of work, much of which she strongly disapproved, she could not but be relieved at anything which would save her father in some degree from the immense strain of work and anxiety, which were now altogether beyond the endurance of a single man, and bid fair to over-tax even Raeburn's giant strength.

Both Charles Osmond and Brian appeared as voluntary witnesses on behalf of the plaintiff, and naturally the first few days of the trial were endurable enough. But on the Friday the defence began, and it became evident that the most bitter spirit would pervade the rest of the proceedings. Mr. Pogson had spared neither trouble nor expense; he had brought witnesses from all the ends of the earth to swear that (in some cases twenty years ago) they had heard the plaintiff speak such and such words or seen him do such and such deeds. The array of witnesses appeared endless; there seemed no reason why the trial ever should come to an end. It bid fair to be a *cause célèbre,* while inevitably Raeburn's notoriety made the public take a great interest in the proceedings. It became the topic of the day. Erica rarely went in any public conveyance without hearing it discussed.

One day she heard the following cheering sentiment.

'Oh, of course you know the jury will never give a verdict for such a fellow as Raeburn.'

'I suppose they can't help being rather prejudiced against him because of his views; but, upon my word, it seems a confounded shame!'

'Oh, I don't see that,' replied the first speaker. 'If he holds such views, he must expect to suffer for them.'

Day after day passed and still the case dragged on. Erica became so accustomed to spending the day in court that at last it seemed to her that she had never done anything else all her life. Every day she hoped that she might be called, longing to get the hateful piece of work over. But days and weeks passed, and still Mr. Cringer and his learned friends examined other witnesses, but kept her in reserve. Mr. Bircham had been exceedingly kind to her, and in the *Daily Review* office, where Erica was treated as a sort of queen, great indignation had been caused by

Mr. Pogson's malice. 'Our little lady' (her sobriquet there) received the hearty support and sympathy of every man in the place, from the editor himself to the printer's devil. Every morning the office-boy brought her in court the allotted work for the day, which she wrote as well as she could during the proceedings or at luncheon-time, with the happy consciousness that all her shortcomings would be set right by the little Irish sub-editor, who worshipped the ground she trod on, and was always ready with courteous and unofficious help.

There were many little pieces of kindness which served to brighten that dreary summer, for Mr. Pogson's ill-advised zeal had stimulated all lovers of justice into a protest against a most glaring instance of bigotry and unfair treatment. Many clergymen spoke out bravely and denounced the defendant's intolerance; many nonconformist ministers risked giving dire offence to their congregations by saying a good word for the plaintiff. Each protest did its modicum of good, but still the weary case dragged on, and every day the bitterness on either side seemed to increase.

Mr. Pogson had, by fair means or foul, induced an enormous number of witnesses to come forward and prove the truth of his statement, and day after day there were the most wearisome references to old diaries, to reports of meetings held in obscure places perhaps more than a dozen years ago, or to some hashed and mangled report of a debate which, incredible though such meanness seems, had been specially constructed by some unscrupulous opponent in such a way as to alter the entire meaning of Raeburn's words—a process which may very easily be effected by a judicious omission of contexts. Raeburn was cheered and encouraged, however, in spite of all the thousand cares and annoyances of that time by the rapidly increasing number of his followers, and by many tokens of most touching devotion from the people for whom, however mistakenly, he had laboured with unwearying patience and zeal. Erica saw only too plainly that Mr. Pogson was, in truth, fighting against Christianity, and every day brought fresh proofs of the injury done to Christ's cause by this modern instance of injustice and religious intolerance.

It was a terribly trying position, and anyone a degree less brave and sincere would probably have lost all faith; but the one visible good effected by that miserable struggle was the strange influence it exerted in developing her character. She was one of those who seem to grow exactly in proportion to the trouble they have had to bear. And so it came to pass that, while evil was wrought in many quarters, in this one good resulted—good not in the least understood by Raeburn, or Aunt Jean, or Tom, who merely knew that Erica was less hot and hasty than in former times, and found it more of a relief than ever to come home to her loving sympathy.

'After all,' they used to say, 'the miserable delusion hasn't been able to spoil her.'

One day, just after the court had re-assembled in the afternoon, Erica was putting the finishing touches to a very sprightly criticism on a certain political speech, when suddenly she heard the name, for which she had waited so long, called in the clerk's most sonorous tones— 'Erica Raeburn!'

She was conscious of a sudden white flash as every face in the crowded court turned towards her, but more conscious of a strong Presence which seemed to wrap her in a calm so perfect that the disagreeable surroundings became a matter of very slight import. Here were hostile eyes indeed; but she was strong enough to face all the powers of evil at once. A sort of murmur ran through the court as she entered the witness-box, but she did not heed it any more than she would have heeded the murmur of the summer wind without. She just stood there strong in her truth and purity, able, if need be, to set a whole world at defiance.

'Pogson's made a mistake in calling her,' said a briefless barrister to one of his companions in adversity; they both spent their lives in hanging about the courts, thankful when they could get a bit of ' deviling.'

'Right you are!' replied the other, putting up his eye-glass to look at Erica, and letting it drop after a brief survey. 'I'd bet twenty to one that girl loses him his case! And I'm hanged if he doesn't deserve to!'

'Well, it is rather a brutal thing to make a man's own child give evidence against him. Hullo! just look at Raeburn! That man's either a consummate actor, or else a living impersonation of righteous anger.'

'No acting there,' replied the other, putting up his eye-glass again. 'It's lucky duelling is a thing of the past, or I expect Pogson would have a bullet in his heart before the day was over. I don't wonder he's furious, poor fellow! Now, then, here's old Cringer working himself up into his very worst temper!'

The whispered dialogue was interrupted for a few minutes, but was continued at intervals.

'By Jove, what a voice she's got! The jury will be flints if they are not influenced by it. Ah, you great brute! I wouldn't have asked her that question for a thousand pounds! How lovely she looks when she blushes! He'll confuse her, though, as sure as fate. No, not a bit of it! That was dignified, wasn't it? How the words rang, "Of course not!" I say, Jack, this will be as good as a lesson in elocution for us!'

'Raeburn looks up at that for the first time! Well, poor devil! however much baited, he can, at any rate, feel proud of his daughter.'

Then came a long pause. For the fire of questions was so sharp that the two would not break the thread by speaking. Once or twice some particularly irritating question was ruled by the judge to be inadmissible, upon which Mr. Cringer looked, in a hesitatingly courteous manner, towards him, and obeyed orders with a smiling deference; then, facing round upon Erica, with a little additional venom, he visited his annoyance upon her by exerting all his unrivalled skill in endeavouring to make her contradict herself.

'You'll make nothing of this one, Cringer,' one of his friends had said to him at the beginning of Erica's evidence. And he had smiled confidently, by way of reply. All the more was he now determined not to be worsted by a young girl, whom he ought to be able to put out of countenance in ten minutes.

The result of this was that, in the words of

the newspaper reports, 'the witness's evidence was not concluded when the court rose.' This was perhaps the greatest part of the trial to Erica. She had hoped, not only for her own, but for her father's, sake that her evidence might all be taken in one day, and Mr. Cringer, while really harming his own cause by prolonging her evidence, inflicted no slight punishment on the most troublesome witness he had ever had to deal with.

The next morning it all came over again, with increased disagreeableness.

'Erica always was the plucky one,' said Tom to his mother, as they watched her enter the witness-box. 'She always did the confessing when we got into scrapes. I only hope that brute of a Cringer won't put her out of countenance.'

He need not have feared, though in truth Erica was tried to the utmost. To begin with, it was one of the very hottest of the dog-days, and the court was crowded to suffocation. This was what the public considered the most interesting day of the trial, for it was the most personal one, and the English have as great a taste for personalites as the Americans, though it is not so constantly gratified. Apparently, Mr. Cringer, being a shrewd man, had managed in the night-watches to calculate Erica's one vulnerable point. She was fatally clear-headed; most aggravatingly and palpably truthful; most unfortunately fascinating; and, though naturally quick-tempered, most annoyingly self-controlled. But she was evidently delicate. If he could sufficiently harass and tire her, he might make her say pretty much what he pleased.

This, at least, was the conclusion at which he had arrived. And if it was indeed his duty to the defendant to exhaust both fair means and foul in the endeavour to win him his case, then he certainly fulfilled his duty. For six long hours, with only a brief interval for luncheon, Erica was baited, badgered, tormented with questions which in themselves were insults, assured that she had said what she had not said; tempted to say what she did not mean, involved in fruitless discussions about places and dates, and, in fact, so thoroughly tortured, that most girls would long before have succumbed. She did not succumb, but she grew whiter and whiter, save when some vile insinuation brought a momentary wave of crimson across her face.

Tom listened breathlessly to the examination, which went on in a constant crescendo of bitterness.

'The plaintiff was in the habit of doing this?'
'Yes.'
'Your suspicion was naturally excited, then?'
'Certainly not.'
'Not excited?'—incredulously.
'Not in the least.'
'You are an inmate of the plaintiff's house, I believe?'
'I am.'
'But this has not always been the case?'
'All my life, with the exception of two years.'
'Your reason for the two years' absence had a connection with the plaintiff's mode of life, had it not?'
'Not in the sense you wish to imply. It had a connection with our extreme poverty.'
'Though an inmate of your father's house, you are often away from home?'
'No, very rarely.'

'Oblige me by giving a straightforward answer. What do you mean by rarely?'

'Very seldom.'

'This is mere equivocation; will you give me a straightforward reply?'

'I can't make it more so,' said Erica, keeping her temper perfectly, and replying to the nagging interrogatories. 'Do you mean once a year, twice a year?' &c., &c., with a steady patience which foiled Mr. Cringer effectually. He opened a fresh subject.

'Do you remember the 1st of September last year?'

'I do.'

'Do you remember what happened then?'

'Partridge-shooting began.'

There was much laughter at this reply; she made it partly because even now the comic side of everything struck her, partly because she wanted to gain time. What in the world was Mr. Cringer driving at?

'Did not something occur that night in Guilford Terrace which you were very anxious to conceal?'

For a moment Erica was dumbfounded. It

flashed upon her that he knew of the Haeberlein adventure, and meant to serve his purpose by distorting it into something very different. Luckily she was almost as rapid a thinker as her father; she saw that there was before her a choice of two evils. She must either allow Mr. Cringer to put an atrocious construction on her unqualified 'yes,' or she must boldly avow Haeberlein's visit.

'With regard to my father there was nothing to conceal,' she replied.

'Will you swear that there was *nothing* to conceal?'

'With regard to my father I swear there was nothing to conceal.'

'Don't bandy words with me. Will you repeat my formula—"Nothing to conceal"?'

'No, I will not repeat that.'

'You admit that there *was* something to conceal?'

'If you call Eric Haeberlein "something,"—yes.'

There was a great sensation in the court at these words. But Mr. Cringer was non-plussed. The mysterious 'something,' out of which he had intended to make such capital, was turned into a boldly avowed reality—a reality which would avail him nothing. Moreover, most people would now see through his very unworthy manœuvre. Furiously he hurled question after question at Erica. He surpassed himself in sheer bullying. By this time, too, she was very weary. The long hours of standing, the insufferable atmosphere, the incessant stabs at her father's character made the examination almost intolerable. And the difficulty of answering the fire of questions was great. She struggled on, however, until the time came when Raeburn stood up to ask whether a certain question was allowable. She looked at him then for the first time, saw how terribly he was feeling her interminable examination, and for a moment lost heart. The rows of people grew hazy and indistinct, Mr. Cringer's face got all mixed up with his wig, she had to hold tightly to the railing. How much longer could she endure!

'Yet you doubtless thought this probable?' continued her tormentor.

'Oh! no, on the contrary, quite the reverse,' said Erica, with a momentary touch of humour.

'Are you acquainted with the popular saying, "None are so blind as those who will not see"?'

The tone was so insulting that indignation restored Erica to her full strength; she was stung into giving a sharp retort.

'Yes,' she said, very quietly. 'It has often occurred to me during this action as strangely applicable to the defendant.'

Mr. Cringer looked as if he could have eaten her. There was a burst of applause, which was speedily suppressed.

'Yet you do not, of course, mean to deny the whole allegation?'

'Emphatically!'

'Are you aware that people will think you either a deluded innocent or an infamous deceiver?'

'I am not here to consider what people may think of me, but to speak the truth.'

And as she spoke she involuntarily glanced towards those twelve fellow-countrymen of hers upon whose verdict so much depended. Probably even the oldest, even the coldest of the jurymen felt his heart beat a little faster as those beautiful, sad, honest eyes scanned the jury-box. As for the counsel for the defence he prudently accepted his defeat, and, as Raeburn would not ask a single question of his daughter in cross-examination, another witness was called.

Long after, it was a favourite story among the young barristers of how Mr. Cringer was checkmated by Raeburn's daughter.

The case dragged on its weary length till August. At last, when two months of the public time had been consumed, when something like £20,000 had been spent, when most bitter resentment had been stirred up amongst the secularists, Mr. Pogson's defence came to an end. Raeburn's reply was short, but effective, and the jury returned a verdict in his favour, fixing the damages, however, at the very lowest sum, not because they doubted that Raeburn had been most grossly libelled, but because the plaintiff had the misfortune to be an atheist.

## CHAPTER VI.

### ROSE'S ADVENTURE.

If Christians would teach Infidels to be just to Christianity, they should themselves be just to infidelity.
JOHN STUART MILL.

THE green-room was one of those rooms which show to most advantage on a winter evening; attractive and comfortable at all times, it nevertheless reached its highest degree of comfort when the dusky green curtains were drawn, when the old wainscotted walls were lighted up by the red glow from the fire, and the well-worn books on the shelves were mellowed by the soft light into a uniform and respectable brown. One November evening, when without was the thickest of London fogs, Erica was sitting at her writing-table with Friskarina on her lap, and Tottie curled up at her feet, hard at work preparing for one of her science classes, when she was interrupted by the sound of a cab drawing up, speedily followed by a loud ring at the bell.

'Surely M. Noirol can't have come already!' she said to herself, looking at her watch. It was just six o'clock, a whole hour before dinner-time. Steps were approaching the door however, and she was just inhospitably wishing her guest elsewhere, when to her intense amazement the servant announced 'Miss Fane-Smith.'

She started forward with an exclamation of incredulity, for it seemed absurd to think of Rose actually coming to see her in her father's house. But incredulity was no longer possible when Rose herself entered, in ulster and travelling hat, with her saucy laughing face, and her invariable content with herself and the world in general.

'Why, Erica!' she cried, kissing her on both cheeks, 'I don't believe you're half properly glad to see me!. Did you think it was my wraith? I assure you it's my own self in the flesh, and very cold flesh too. What a delightful room! I'd no idea atheists' homes were so much like other people's. You cold-hearted little cousin, why don't you welcome me?'

'I am very glad to see you,' said Erica, kissing her again. 'But, Rose, what did bring you here?'

'A fusty old cab, a four-wheeler, a growler, don't you call them? But, if you knew why I have come to you in this unexpected way, you would treat me like the heroine I am, and not stand there like an incarnation of prudent hesitation. I've been treated like the man in the parable, I've fallen among thieves, and am left with my raiment, certainly, but not a farthing besides in the world. And now, of course, you'll enact the good Samaritan.'

'Come and get warm,' said Erica, drawing a chair towards the fire, but still feeling uncomfortable at the idea of Mr. Fane-Smith's horror and dismay could he have seen his daughter's situation. 'How do you come to be in town, Rose, and where were you robbed?'

'Why, I was going to stay with the Alburys at Sandgale, and left home about three, but at Paddington, when I went to get my ticket, lo and behold, my purse had disappeared, and I was left lamenting, like Lord Ullin in the song!'

'Have you any idea who took it?'

'Yes, I rather think it must have been a man on the Paddington platform who walked with a limp. I remember his pushing up against me very roughly, and I expect that was when he took it. The porters were all horrid about it, though; I could get no one to help me, and I hadn't even the money to get my ticket. At last an old lady, who had heard of my penniless condition, advised me to go to any friends I might happen to have in London, and I bethought me of my cousin Erica. You will befriend me, won't you? For it is simply impossible to get to Sandgale to-night; there is no other train stopping there.'

'I wish I knew what was right,' said Erica, looking much perplexed. 'You see, Rose, I'm afraid Mr. Fane-Smith would not like you to come here.'

'Oh, nonsense,' said Rose, laughing. 'He couldn't mind in such a case as this. Why, I can't stay in the street all night. Besides, he doesn't know anything about your home, how should he?'

This was true enough, but still Erica hesitated.

'Who was that white-haired, patriarchal-looking man whom I met in the hall?' asked Rose. 'A sort of devotional quaker kind of man.'

Erica laughed aloud at this description.

'That's my father!' she said; and, before she had quite recovered her gravity, Raeburn came into the room with some papers which he wanted copied.

'Father,' said Erica. 'This is Rose, and she has come to ask our help because her purse has been stolen at Paddington, and she is stranded in London with no money.'

'It sounds dreadfully like begging,' said Rose, looking up into the brown eyes which seemed half kindly, half critical.

They smiled at this, and became at once only kind and hospitable.

'Not in the least,' he said; 'I am very glad you came to us.'

And then he began to ask her many practical questions about her adventure, ending by promising to put the matter at once into the hands of the police. They were just discussing the impossibility of getting to Sandgale that evening, when Tom came into the room.

'Where is mother?' he asked. 'She has kept her cab at the door at least ten minutes; I had to give the fellow an extra sixpence.'

'That wasn't auntie's cab,' said Erica. 'She came home half an hour ago; it was Rose's cab. I hope you didn't send away her boxes?'

'I beg your pardon,' said Tom, looking much surprised and a little amused. 'The boxes are safe in the hall, but I'm afraid the cab is gone beyond recall.'

'You see it is evidently meant that I should quarter myself upon you!' said Rose, laughing.

Upon which Raeburn, with a grave and slightly repressive courtesy, said they should be very happy if she would stay with them.

'That will make my adventure perfect!' said Rose, her eyes dancing.

At which Raeburn smiled again, amused to think of the uneventful life in which such a trifling incident could seem an 'adventure.'

'It seems very inhospitable,' said Erica; 'but don't you think, Rose, you had better go back to Greyshot?'

'No, you tiresome piece of prudence, I don't,' said Rose, perversely. 'And what's more, I won't, as Uncle Luke has asked me to stay.'

Erica felt very uncomfortable; she could have spoken decidedly had she been alone with any of the three, but she could not, before them all, say 'Mr. Fane-Smith thinks father an incarnation of wickedness, and would be horrified if he knew that you were here.'

Tom had in the meantime walked to the window and drawn aside the curtain.

'The weather means to settle the question for you,' he said. 'You simply can't go off in such a fog as this; it would take you hours to get to Paddington, if you ever did get there, which is doubtful.'

They looked out and saw that he had not exaggerated matters; the fog had grown much worse since Rose's arrival, and it had been bad enough then to make travelling by no means safe. Erica saw that there was no help for it. Mr. Fane-Smith's anger must be incurred, and Rose must stay with them. She went away to see that her room was prepared, and coming back a little later found that in that brief time Rose had managed to enthrall poor Tom, who, not being used to the genus, was very easily caught, his philosophy being by no means proof against a fair-haired, bright-looking girl, who in a very few moments made him feel that she thought most highly of him, and cared as no one had ever cared before for his opinion. She had not the smallest intention of doing harm, but admiration was what she lived for, and to flirt with every man she met had become almost as natural and necessary to her as to breathe.

Erica, out of loyalty to Mr. Fane-Smith, and regard for Tom's future happiness, felt bound to be hard-hearted and to separate them at dinner. Tom used to sit at the bottom of the table, as Raeburn did not care for the trouble of carving; Erica was at the head with her father in his usual place at her right hand. She put Rose in between him and the professor, who generally dined with them on Saturday; upon the opposite side were Aunt Jean and Monsieur Noirol. Now Rose, who had been quite in her element as long as she had been talking with Tom in the green-room, felt decidedly out of her element when she was safely ensconced between her white-haired uncle and the shaggy-looking professor. If Erica had felt bewildered when first introduced to the gossip and small 'society' talk of Greyshot, Rose felt doubly bewildered when for the first time in her life she came into a thoroughly scientific atmosphere. She realised that there were a few things which she had yet to learn. She was not fond of learning, so the discovery was the reverse of pleasant; she felt ignorant and humbled, liking to be *au fait* at everything and to know things and do things just a little better than other people. Having none of the humility of a true learner, she only felt annoyed at her own ignorance, not raised and bettered and stimulated by a glimpse of the infinite greatness of science.

Raeburn, seeing that she was not in the least

interested in the discussion of the future of electricity, left the professor to continue it with Tom, and began to talk to her about the loss of her purse, and to tell her of various losses which he had had. But Rose had the mortifying consciousness that all the time he talked he was listening to the conversation between Erica and Monsieur Noirol. As far as Rose could make out, it was on French politics; but they spoke so fast that her indifferent school French was of very little service to her. By-and-by Raeburn was drawn into the discussion, and Rose was left to amuse herself as well as she could by listening to a rapid flow of unintelligible French on one side, and to equally unintelligible scientific talk on the other. By-and-by this was merged into a discussion on some recent book. They seemed to get deeply interested in a dispute as to whether Spinoza was or was not at any time in his life a Cartesian.

Rose really listened to this for want of something better to do, and Raeburn, thinking that he had been neglecting her, and much relieved at the thought that he had at length found some point of mutual interest, asked her whether she had read the book in question.

'Oh, I have no time for reading,' said Rose.

He looked a little amused at this statement. Rose continued—

'Who was Spinoza? I never heard any of his music.'

'He was a philosopher, not a composer,' said Raeburn, keeping his countenance with difficulty.

'What dreadfully learned people you are!' said Rose, with one of her arch smiles. 'But do tell me, how can a man be a Cartesian? I've heard of Cartesian wells, but never——'

She broke off, for this was quite too much for Raeburn's gravity; he laughed, but so pleasantly that she laughed too.

'You are thinking of artesian wells, I fancy,' he said, in his kindly voice; and he began to give her a brief outline of Descartes philosophy, which it is to be feared she did not at all appreciate. She was not sorry when Erica appealed to him for some disputed fact, in which they all seemed most extraordinarily interested, for when the discussion had lasted some minutes, Tom went off in the middle of dinner and fetched in two or three bulky books of reference; these were eagerly seized upon, to the entire disregard of the pudding, which was allowed to get cold.

Presently the very informal meal was ended by some excellent coffee in the place of the conventional dessert, after which came a hurried dispersion, as they were all going to some political meeting at the East-end. Cabs were unattainable, and, having secured a couple of link-boys, they set off, apparently in excellent spirits.

'Fancy turning out on such a night as this!' said Rose, putting her arm within Erica's. 'I am so glad you are not going, for now we can really have a cosy talk. I've ever so much to tell you.'

Erica looked rather wistfully after the torches and the retreating forms as they made their way down the steps; she was much disappointed at being obliged to miss this particular meeting, but luckily Rose was not in the least likely to find this out, for she could not imagine for a moment that anyone really cared about missing a political meeting, particularly when it would have involved turning out on such a disagreeable night.

Erica had persuaded Rose to telegraph both to her friends at Sandgale and to her mother, to tell of her adventure, and to say that she would go on to Sandgale on the Monday. For, unfortunately, the next day was Sunday, and Rose looked so aghast at the very idea of travelling then that Erica could say nothing more, though she surmised rightly enough that Mr. Fane-Smith would have preferred even Sunday travelling to a Sunday spent in Luke Raeburn's house. There was evidently, however, no help for it. Rose was there, and there she must stay; all that Erica could do was to keep her as much as might be out of Tom's way, and to beg the others not to discuss any subjects bearing on their anti-religious work; and, since there was not the smallest temptation to try to make Rose a convert to Secularism, they were all quite willing to avoid such topics.

But, in spite of all her care, Erica failed most provokingly that day. To begin with, Rose pleaded a headache, and would not go with her to the early service. Erica was disappointed; but when, on coming home, she found Rose in the dining-room, comfortably chatting over the fire to Tom, who was evidently in the seventh heaven of happiness, she felt as if she could have shaken them both. By-and-by she tried to give Tom a hint, which he did not take at all kindly.

'Women never like to see another woman admired,' he replied, with a sarcastic smile.

'But, Tom,' she pleaded, 'her father would be so dreadfully angry if he saw the way you go on with her.'

'Oh, shut up, do, about her father!' said Tom, crossly. 'You have crammed him down our throats quite enough.'

It was of no use to say more; but she went away feeling sore and ruffled. She was just about to set off with Rose to Charles Osmond's church, when the door of the study was hastily opened.

'Have you seen the last *Longstaff Mercury?*' said Raeburn, in the voice which meant that he was worried and much pressed for time.

'It was in here yesterday,' said Erica.

'Then, Tom, you must have moved it,' said Raeburn, sharply. 'It's a most provoking thing; I specially wanted to quote from it.'

'I've not touched it,' said Tom. 'It's those servants; they never can leave the papers alone.'

He was turning over the contents of a paper-rack, evidently not in the best of tempers. Rose sprang forward.

'Let me help,' she said, with one of her irresistible smiles.

Erica felt more provoked than she would have cared to own. It was very clear that those two would never find anything.

'Look here, Erica,' said Raeburn, 'do see if it isn't upstairs. Tom is a terrible hand at finding things.'

So she searched in every nook and cranny of the house, and at last found the torn remains of the paper in the housemaid's cupboard. The rest of it had been used for lighting a fire.

Raeburn was a good deal annoyed.

'Surely, my dear, such things might be prevented,' he said, not crossly, but in the sort of forbearing, expostulatory tone which a woman dislikes more than anything, specially if she happens to be a careful housekeeper.

'I told you it was your servants!' said Tom, triumphantly.

'They've had orders again and again not to touch the newspapers,' said Erica.

'Well, come along, Tom,' said Raeburn, taking up his hat. 'We are very late.'

They drove off, and Erica and Rose made the best of their way to church, to find the service begun, and seats unattainable. Rose was very good-natured, however, about the standing. She began faintly to perceive that Erica did not lead the easiest of lives; also she saw, with a sort of wonder, what an influence she was in the house, and how, notwithstanding their difference in creed, she was always ready to meet the others on every point where it was possible to do so. Rose could not help thinking of a certain friend of hers, who, having become a ritualist, never lost an opportunity of emphasising the difference between her own views and the views of her family; and of Kate Righton at Greyshot, who had adopted the most rigid evangelical views, and treated her good old father and mother as 'worldly' and 'unconverted' people.

In the afternoon Tom had it all his own way. Raeburn was in his study preparing for his evening lecture; Mrs. Craigie had a Bible class at the East-end, in which she showed up the difficulties and contradictions of the old and new testaments; Erica had a Bible class in Charles Osmond's parish, in which she tried to explain the same difficulties. Rose was therefore alone in the green-room, and perfectly ready to attract Tom and keep him spell-bound for the afternoon. It is quite possible, however, that no great harm would have been done, if the visit had come to a natural end the following day; Rose would certainly have thought no more of Tom, and Tom might very possibly have come to his senses when she was no longer there to fascinate him. But on the Sunday evening when the toils of the day were over, and they were all enjoying the restful home quiet which did not come very often in their busy lives, Rose's visit was brought to an abrupt close.

Looked at by an impartial spectator, the green-room would surely have seemed a model of family peace and even of Sunday restfulness. Rose was sitting at the piano playing Mendelssohn's 'Christmas Pieces,' and giving great pleasure to everyone, for art was in this house somewhat overshadowed by science, and it did not very often happen that they could listen to such playing as Rose's, which was for that reason a double pleasure. Tom was sitting near her looking supremely peaceful. On one side of the fireplace Mrs. Craigie and Mrs. MacNaughton were playing their weekly game of chess. On the other side Raeburn had his usual Sunday evening recreation, his microscope. Erica knelt beside him, her auburn head close to his white one as they arranged their specimens or consulted books of reference. The professor, who had looked in on his way home from the lecture to borrow a review, was browsing contentedly among the books on the table, with the comfortable sense that he might justifiably read in a desultory holiday fashion.

It was upon this peaceful and almost Sabbatical group that a disturbing element entered in the shape of Mr. Fane-Smith. He stood for an instant at the door, taking in the scene, or rather taking that superficial view which the narrow-minded usually take. He was shocked at the chess-men; shocked at that profane microscope, and those week-day sections of plants; shocked at the music, though he must have heard it played as a voluntary on many church organs, and not only shocked, but furious, at finding his daughter in a very nest of secularists.

Everyone seemed a little taken aback when he entered. He took no notice whatever of Raeburn, but went straight up to Rose.

'Go and put on your things at once,' he said, 'I have come to take you home.'

'Oh, papa,' began Rose, 'how you——'

'Not a word, Rose. Go and dress, and don't keep me waiting.'

Erica, with a vain hope of making Mr. Fane-Smith behave at least civilly, came forward and shook hands with him.

'I don't think you have met my father before,' she said.

Raeburn had come a few steps forward; Mr.

Fane-Smith inclined his head about a quarter of an inch; Raeburn bowed, then said to Erica,

'Perhaps Mr. Fane-Smith would prefer waiting in my study.'

'Thanks, I will wait where I am,' said Mr. Fane-Smith, pointedly ignoring the master of the house, and addressing Erica. 'Thank you,' as she offered him a chair, ' I prefer to stand. Have the goodness to see that Rose is quick.'

'Thinks the chairs atheistical!' remarked Tom, to himself.

Raeburn, looking a degree more stately than usual, stood on the hearthrug with his back to the fire, not in the least forgiving his enemy, but merely adopting for himself the most dignified *rôle*. Mr. Fane-Smith a few paces off with his anger and ill-concealed contempt did not show to advantage. Something in the relative sizes of the two struck the professor as comically like Landseer's 'Dignity and Impudence.' He would have smiled at the thought had he not been very angry at the discourteous treatment his friend was receiving. Mrs. MacNaughton sat with her queen in her hand as though meditating her next move, but in reality absorbed in watching the game played by the living chess-men before her. Tom at last broke the uncomfortable silence by asking the professor about some of Erica's specimens, and at length Rose came down, much to everyone's relief, followed by Erica, who had been helping her to collect her things.

'Are you ready?' said her father. 'Then come at once.'

'Let me at least say good-bye, papa,' said Rose, very angry at being forced to make this undignified, and, as she rightly felt, rude exit.

'Come at once,' said Mr. Fane-Smith, in an inexorable voice. As he left the room, he turned and bowed stiffly.

'Go down and open the door for them, Tom,' said Raeburn, who throughout Mr. Fane-Smith's visit had maintained a stern, stately silence.

Tom, nothing loth, obeyed. Erica was already half-way downstairs with the guests, but he caught them up, and managed to say good-bye to Rose, even to whisper a hope that they might meet again, to which Rose replied with a charming blush and smile, which, Tom flattered himself, meant that she really cared for him.

Had Rose gone quietly away the next morning, he would not have been goaded into any such folly. A cab was waiting; but, when Rose was once inside it, her father recovered his power of speech, and turned upon Erica as they stood by the front door.

'I should have thought,' he said, in an angry voice, 'that, after our anxiety to persuade you to leave your home, you might have known that I should never allow Rose to enter this hell, to mix with blaspheming atheists, to be contaminated by vile infidels!'

Erica's Highland hospitality and strong family loyalty were so outraged by the words, that to keep silence was impossible.

'You forget to whom you are speaking!' she said, quickly. 'You forget that this is my father's house!'

'I would give a great deal to be able to forget,' said Mr. Fane-Smith. 'I have tried to deal kindly with you, tried to take you from this accursed place, and you repay me by tempting Rose to stay with you!'

Erica had recovered herself by this time. Tom, watching her, could not but wonder at her self-restraint. She did not retaliate, did not even attempt to justify her conduct; at such a a moment words would have been worse than useless. But Tom, while fully appreciating the common-sense of the non-resistance, was greatly astonished. Was this his old playmate who had always had the most deliciously aggravating retort ready? Was this hot-tempered Erica? That Mr. Fane-Smith's words were hurting her very much he could see; he guessed, too, that the consciousness that he, a secularist, was looking on at this unfortunate display of Christian intolerance, added a sting to her grief.

'It is useless to profess Christianity,' stormed Mr. Fane-Smith. 'If you openly encourage infidelity by consorting with these blasphemers, you are no Christian! A mere socinian—a latitudinarian!'

Erica's lips quivered a little at this; but she remembered that Christ had been called harder names still by religious bigots of his day, and she kept silence.

'But understand this,' continued Mr. Fane-Smith, 'that I approve less than ever of your intimacy with Rose, and until you come to see your folly in staying here, your worse than folly—your deliberate choice of home and refusal to put religious duty first—there had better be no more intercourse between us.'

'Can you indeed think that religious duty ever requires a child to break the fifth commandment?' said Erica, with no anger, but with a certain sadness in her tone. 'Can you really think that by leaving my father I should be pleasing a perfectly loving God?'

'You lean entirely on your own judgment!' said Mr. Fane-Smith; 'if you were not too proud to be governed by authority, you would see that precedent shows you to be entirely in the wrong. St. John rushed from the building polluted by the heretic Cerinthus, a man who, compared with your father, was almost orthodox!'

Erica smiled faintly.

'If that story is indeed true, I should think he remembered before long a reproof his intolerance brought him once. "Ye know not what spirit ye are of." And really, if we are to fall back upon tradition, I may quote the story of Abraham turning the unbeliever out of his tent on a stormy night. "I have suffered him these hundred years," was the Lord's reproof, "though he dishonoured me, and couldest not thou endure him for one night!" I am sorry to distress you, but I must do what I know to be right.'

'Don't talk to me of right,' exclaimed Mr. Fane-Smith, with a shudder. 'You are wilfully putting your blaspheming father before Christ. But I see my words are wasted. Let me pass! The air of this house is intolerable to me!'

He hurried away, his anger flaming up again, when Tom followed him, closing the door of the cab with punctilious politeness. Rose was frightened.

'Oh, papa,' she said, trembling, 'why are you so angry? You haven't been scolding Erica about it? If there was any fault anywhere, the fault was mine. What did you say to her, papa? What have you been doing?'

Mr. Fane-Smith was in that stage of anger when it is pleasant to repeat all one's hot words to a second audience, and, moreover, he wanted to impress Rose with the enormity of her visit. He repeated all that he had said to Erica, interspersed with yet harder words about her perverse self-reliance and disregard for authority.

Rose listened, but at the end she trembled no longer. She had in her a bit of the true Raeburn nature, with its love of justice and its readiness to stand up for the oppressed.

'Papa,' she said, all her spoilt-child manners and little affectations giving place to the most perfect earnestness. 'Papa, you must forgive me for contradicting you, but you are indeed very much mistaken. I may have been silly to go there. Erica did try all she could to persuade me to go back to Greyshot yesterday; but I am glad I stayed, even though you are so angry about it. If there is a noble, brave girl on earth, it is Erica! You don't know what she is to them all, and how they all love her. I will tell you what this visit has done for me. It has made me ashamed of myself, and I am going to try to be wiser, and less selfish.'

It was something of an effort to Rose to say this, but she had been very much struck with the sight of Erica's home-life, and she wanted to prove to her father how greatly he had misjudged her cousin. Unfortunately, there are some people in this world who, having once got an idea into their heads, will keep it in the teeth of the very clearest evidence to the contrary.

In the meantime, Tom had rejoined Erica in the hall.

'How can such a brute have such a daughter?' he said. 'Never mind, *Cugina*, you were a little brick, and treated him much better than he deserved. If that is a Christian, and this a latitudinarian, and all the other heresies he threw at your head, all I can say is, commend me to your sort, and may I never have the misfortune to encounter another of his!'

Erica did not reply; she felt too sick at heart. She walked slowly upstairs, trying to stifle the weary longing for Brian, which, though very often present, became a degree less bearable when her isolated position—between two fires, as it were—had been specially emphasized.

'That's a nice specimen of Christian charity!' said Aunt Jean, as they returned to the greenroom.

'And he set upon Erica at the door, and hurled hard names at her as fast as he could go,' said Tom, proceeding to give a detailed account of Mr. Fane-Smith's parting utterances.

Erica picked up Tottie, and held him closely, turning, as all lovers of animals do in times of trouble, to the comforting devotion of those dumb friends who do not season their love with curiosity or unasked advice, or that pity which is less sympathetic than silence, and burdens us with the feeling that our sad 'case' will be gossiped over in the same pitying tones at afternoon teas and morning calls. Tottie could not gossip, but he could talk to her with his bright brown eyes, and do something to fill a great blank in her life.

Tom's account of the scene in the hall made everyone angry.

'And yet,' said Mrs. MacNaughton, 'these Christians, who use of us such language as this, own as their master one who taught that a mere angry word which wounded a neighbour should receive severe punishment!'

Raeburn said nothing, only watched Erica keenly. She was leaning against the mantelpiece, her eyes very sad looking, and about her face that expression of earnest listening which is characteristic of those who are beginning to learn the true meaning of humility and 'righteous judgment.' She had pushed back the thick waves of hair which usually overshadowed her forehead, and looked something between a lion with a tangled mane and a saint with a halo.

'Never mind,' said the professor, cheerfully, 'it is to bigotry like this that we shall owe our recovery of Erica. And seriously, what can you think of a religion which can make a man behave like this to one who had never injured him, who, on the contrary, had befriended his child.'

'It is not Christ's religion which teaches him to do it,' said Erica, ' it is the perversion of that religion.'

'Then in all conscience the perversion is vastly more powerful and extended than what you deem the reality.'

'Unfortunately yes,' said Erica, sighing. 'At present it is.'

'At present!' retorted the professor, 'why, you have had more than eighteen hundred years to improve in.'

'You yourself taught me to have patience with the slow processes of Nature,' said Erica, smiling a little. 'If you allow unthinkable ages for the perfecting of a layer of rocks, do you wonder that in a few hundred years a church is still far from perfect?'

'I expect perfection in no human being,' said the professor, taking up a Bible from the table and turning over the pages with the air of a man who knew its contents well: 'when I see Christians in some sort obeying this, I will believe that their system is the true system; but not before.' He guided his finger slowly beneath the following lines: '" Let all bitterness, and wrath, and anger, and clamour, and evil-speaking be put away from you, with all malice." There is the precept, you see, and a very good precept to be found in the secularist creed as well; but now let us look at the practice. See how we secularists are treated! why, we live as it were in a foreign land, compelled to keep the law yet denied the protection of the law!—"Outlaws of the constitution, outlaws of the human race," as Burke was kind enough to call us. No! when I see Christians no longer slandering our leaders, no longer coining hateful lies about us out of their own evil imaginations, when I see equal justice shown to all men of whatever creed, then, and not till then, will I listen to all those lofty assertions about the all-conquering love. Christianity has yet to prove itself the religion of love; at present it is the religion of exclusion.'

Mrs. MacNaughton, who was exceedingly fond of Erica, looked sorry for her.

'You see, Erica,' she said, 'the professor judges by averages. No one would deny that some of the greatest men in the world have been, and are even in the present day, Christians; they have been brought up in it, and can't free themselves from its trammels. You have a few people like the Osmonds, a few really liberal men; but you have only to see how they are treated by their *confrères* to realise the illiberality of the religion as a whole.'

'I think with you,' said Erica, 'that if the revelation of God's love, and His purpose for all, be only to be learnt from the lives of Christians, it is a bad look-out for us. But God *has* given us one perfect revelation of Himself, and the perfect Son can make us see plainly even when the imperfect sons are holding up to us a distorted likeness of the Father.'

She had spoken quietly, but with the tremulousness of strong feeling, and, moreover, she was so sensitive that the weight of the hostile atmosphere oppressed her, and made speaking a great difficulty. When she had ended, she turned away from the disapproving eyes to the only sympathetic eyes in the room—the dog's. They looked up into hers with that wistful endeavour to understand the meaning of something beyond their grasp, which makes the eyes of animals so pathetic.

There was a silence; her use of the adjective 'perfect' had been very trying to all her hearers, who strongly disapproved of the whole sentence; but then she was so evidently sincere and so thoroughly loveable that no one liked to give her pain.

Aunt Jean was the only person who thought there was much chance of her ever returning to the ranks of secularism; she was the only one who spoke now.

'Well, well,' she said, pityingly, 'you are but

young; you will think very differently ten years hence.'

Erica kept back an angry retort with difficulty, and Raeburn, whose keen sense of justice was offended, instantly came forward in her defence, though her words had been like a fresh stab in the old wound.

'That is no argument, Jean,' he said, quickly. 'It is the very unjust extinguisher which the elders use for the suppression of individuality in the young.'

As he spoke, he readjusted a slide in his microscope, making it plain to all that he intended the subject to be dropped. He had a wonderful way of impressing his individuality on others, and the household settled down once more into the Sabbatical calm which had been broken by a bigoted Sabbatarian.

Nothing more was heard of Rose, nor did Erica have an opportunity of talking over the events of that Sunday with her father for some days, for he was exceedingly busy, the long weeks wasted during the summer in the wearisome libel case having left upon his hands vast arrears of provincial work. In some of the large iron foundries you may see hundreds of different machines all kept in action by a forty horse-power engine; and Raeburn was the great motive-power which gave life to all the branches of Raeburnites which now stretched throughout the length and breadth of the land. Without him they would have relapsed, very probably, into that fearfully wide-spread mass of indifference which is not touched by any form of Christianity or religious revival, but which had responded to the practical, secular teaching of the singularly powerful secularist leader. He had a wonderful gift of stirring up the heretofore indifferent, and making them take a really deep interest in national questions. This was by far the happiest part of his life, because it was the healthy part of it. The sameness of his anti-theological work, and the barrenness of mere down-pulling, were distasteful enough to him; he was often heartily sick of it all, and had he not thought it a positive duty to attack what he deemed a very mischievous delusion, he would gladly have handed over this part of his work to some one else, and devoted himself entirely to national work.

He had been away from home for several days lecturing in the north of England. Erica was not expecting his return till the following day, when one evening a telegram was brought in to her. It was from her father to this effect:

'*Expect me home by mail train about two a.m. Place too hot to hold me.*'

He had now to a great extent lived down the opposition which had made lecturing in his younger days a matter of no small risk to life and limb; but Erica knew that there were reasons which made the people of Ashborough particularly angry with him just now. Ashborough was one of those strange towns which can never be depended upon. It was renowned for its riots, and was, in fact (to use a slang word) a 'rowdy' place. More than once in the old days Raeburn had been roughly handled there, and Erica bore a special grudge to it, for it was the scene of her earliest recollection—one of those dark pictures which, having been indelibly traced on the heart of a child, influence the whole character and the future life far more than some people think.

It was perhaps that old memory which made

her waiting so anxious that evening. Moreover, she had at first no one to talk to, which made it much worse. Aunt Jean had gone to bed with a bad toothache, and must on no account be disturbed; and Tom had suddenly announced his intention that morning of going down to Brighton on his bicycle, and had set off, rather to Erica's dismay, since, in a letter to Charles Osmond, Donovan happened to have mentioned that the Fane-Smiths had taken a house there for six weeks. She hated herself for being suspicious; but Tom had been so unlike himself since Rose's visit, and it was such an unheard-of thing that he should take a day's holiday during her father's absence, that it was scarcely possible to avoid drawing the natural inference. She was very unhappy about him, but did not of course feel justified in saying a word to anyone else about the matter. Charles Osmond happened to look in for a moment later on, expecting to find Raeburn at home, and then in her relief she did give him an account of the unfortunate Sunday, though avoiding all mention of Tom.

'It was just like you to come at the very time I was wanting some one to talk to,' she said, sitting down in her favourite nook on the hearth-rug with Friskie on her lap. 'Not a word has been said of that miserable Sunday since, though I'm afraid a good deal has been thought. After all, you know, there was a ludicrous side to it as well. I shall never forget the look of them all when Rose and I came down again: Mr. Fane-Smith standing there by the table the very incarnation of contemptuous anger, and father just here, looking like a tired thunder-cloud! But, though one laughs at one aspect of it, one could cry one's eyes out over the thing as a whole—indeed, just now I find myself agreeing with Mr. Tulliver that it's "a puzzling world."'

'The fact is,' said Charles Osmond, 'that you consent patiently enough to share God's pain over those who don't believe in Him; but you grumble sorely at finding a lack of charity in the world; yet that pain is God's too.'

'Yes,' sighed Erica; 'but somehow from Christians it seems so hard!'

'Quite true, child,' he replied, half absently. 'It is hard—most hard. But don't let it make you uncharitable, Erica. You are sharing God's pain, but remember it is only His perfect love which makes that pain bearable.'

'I do find it hard to love bigots,' said Erica, sighing. 'They! What do they know about the thousand difficulties which have driven people into Secularism? If they could but see that they and their narrow theories and their false distortions of Christ's gospel are the real cause of it all, there would be some hope! But they either can't see it or won't.'

'My dear, we're all a lot of blind puppies together,' said Charles Osmond. 'We tumble up against each other just for want of eyes. We shall see when we get to the end of the nine days, you know.'

'You see now,' said Erica; 'you never hurt us, and rub us the wrong way.'

'Perhaps not,' he replied, laughing. 'But Mr. Roberts and some of my other brethren would tell a different tale. By-the-by, would you care to help another befogged mortal who is in the region you are safely out of? The evolution theory is the difficulty, and, if you have time to enter into his trouble, I think you could help him much better than I can. If I could see him, I might tackle him; but I can't do it on paper. You could, I think; and, as the fellow lives at the other side of the world, one can do nothing except by correspondence.'

Erica was delighted to undertake the task, and she was particularly well-fitted for it. Perhaps no one is really qualified for the post of a clearer of doubts who has not himself faced and conquered doubts of a similar nature.

So there was a new interest for her on that long, lonely evening, and, as she waited for her father's return, she had time to think out quietly the various points which she would first take up. By-and-by she slept a little, and then, in the silence of the night, crept down to the lower regions to add something to the tempting little supper which she had ready in the green-room. But time crept on, and in the silence she could hear dozens of clocks telling each hour, and the train had been long due, and still her father did not come.

At last she became too anxious to read or

think to any purpose; she drew aside the curtain, and, in spite of the cold, curled herself up on the window-seat, with her face pressed close to the glass. Watching, in a literal sense, was impossible, for there was a dense fog, if possible, worse than the fog of the preceding Saturday, but she had the feeling that to be by the window made her in some unaccountable way nearer to her father, and it certainly had the effect of showing her that there was a very good reason for unpunctuality.

The old square was as quiet as death. Once a policeman raised her hopes for a minute by pacing slowly up the pavement; but he passed on, and all was still once more, except that every now and then the furniture in the room creaked, making the eerie stillness all the more noticeable. Erica began to shiver a little, more from apprehension than from cold. She wished the telegram had come from any other town in England, and tried in vain not to conjure up a hundred horrible visions of possible catastrophes. At length she heard steps in the distance, and straining her eyes to penetrate the thick darkness of the murky night, was able to make out just beneath the window a sort of yellow glare. She ran downstairs at full speed to open the door, and there upon the step stood a link-boy, the tawny light from his torch showing up to perfection the magnificent proportions of the man in a shaggy, brown Inverness who stood beside him, and bringing into strong relief the masses of white hair and the rugged Scottish face, which, spite of cold and great weariness, bore its usual expression of philosophic calm.

'I thought you were never coming,' said Erica. 'Why, you must be half frozen! What a night it is!'

'We've been more than an hour groping our way from the station,' said Raeburn; 'and cabs were unattainable.' Then, turning to the link-boy, 'Come in; you are as cold and hungry as I am. Have you got something hot, Eric?'

'Soup and coffee,' said Erica. 'Which would he like best?'

The boy gave his vote for soup, and, having seen him thoroughly satisfied and well-paid, they sent him home, and to his dying day he was proud to tell the story of the foggy night when the people's tribune had given him half his own supper. The father and daughter were soon comfortably installed beside the green-room fire, Raeburn making a hearty meal, though it was past three o'clock.

'I never dreamt of finding you up, little son Eric,' he said, when the warmth and the food had revived him. 'I only telegraphed for fear you should lock up for the night and leave me to shiver unknown on the door-step.'

'But what happened?' asked Erica. 'Why couldn't you lecture?'

'Ashborough had worked itself up into one of its tumults, and the fools of authorities thought it would excite a breach of the peace, which was excited quite as much and probably more by my not lecturing. But I'm not going to be beaten! I shall go down there again in a few weeks.'

'Was there any rioting?'

'Well, there was a roughish mob, who prevented my eating my dinner in peace, and pursued me even into my bed-room; and some of the Ashborough lambs were kind enough to overturn my cab as I was going to the station. But, having escaped with nothing worse than a shaking, I'll forgive them for that. The fact is, they had burnt me in effigy on the 5th, and had so much enjoyed the ceremony that when the original turned up they really couldn't be civil to him, it would have been so very tame. I'm told the effigy was such a fearful-looking monster that it frightened the bairnies out of their wits, specially as it was first carried all round the place on a parish coffin!'

'What a hateful plan that effigy-burning is!' said Erica. 'Were you not really hurt at all when they upset your cab?'

'Perhaps a little bruised,' said Raeburn, 'and somewhat angry with my charitable opponents. I didn't so much mind being overturned, but I hate being baulked. They shall have the lecture, however, before long; I'm not going to be beaten. On the whole, they couldn't have chosen a worse night for their little game. I seriously thought we never should grope our way home through that fog. It has quite taken me back to my young days when this sort of thing met one on every hand; and there was no little daughter to cheer me up then, and very often no supper, either.'

'That was when you were living in Blank Street.'

'Yes, in a room about the size of a sentry box. It was bearable all except the black-beetles! I've never seen such beetles before or since—twice the size of the ordinary ones. I couldn't convince the landlady that they even existed, she always maintained that they never rose to the attics; but one night I armed myself with Cruden's concordance, and, thanks to its weight and my good aim, killed six at a time, and produced the corpses as evidence. I shall never forget the good lady's face! "You see, sir," she said, "they never come by day; they 'ates the light, because their deeds is evil."'

'Were the beetles banished after that?' asked Erica, laughing.

'No, they went on to the bitter end,' said Raeburn, with one of his bright, humorous looks. 'And I believe the landlady put it all down to my atheistical views—a just retribution for harbouring such a notorious fellow in her house! But there, my child, we mustn't sit up any longer gossiping; run off to bed. I'll see that the lights are all out.'

## CHAPTER VII.

### DREEING OUT THE INCH.

Scepticism for that century, we must consider as the decay of old ways of believing, the preparation afar off for new, better, and wider ways—an inevitable thing. We will not blame men for it; we will lament their hard fate. We will understand that destruction of old forms is not destruction of everlasting substances; that scepticism, as sorrowful and hateful as we see it, is not an end but a beginning.

CARLYLE.

ONE June evening, an elderly man, with closely-cropped iron-grey hair, might have been seen in a certain railway-carriage as the Folkestone train reached its destination. The Cannon Street platform was, as usual, the scene of bustle and confusion, most of the passengers were met by friends or relatives, others formed a complete party in themselves, and, with the exception of the elderly man, there was scarcely a unit among them. The fact of his loneliness would not, of course, have been specially remarkable had it not been that he was evidently in the last stage of some painful illness; he was also a foreigner, and, not being accustomed to the English luggage system, he had failed to secure a porter as the train drew up, and so, while others were fighting their way to the van, he, who needed assistance more than any of them, was left to shift for himself. He moved with great difficulty, dragging down from the carriage a worn black bag, and occasionally muttering to himself, not as a peevish invalid would have done, but as if it were a sort of solace to his loneliness,

'The hardest day I've had, this! If I had but my *Herzblättchen* now, how quickly she would pilot me through this throng. Ah, well! having managed to do the rest, I'll not be beaten by this last bit. *Potztausend!* these English are all elbows!'

He frowned with pain as the self-seeking crowd pushed and jostled him, but never once lost his temper, and at length, after long waiting, his turn came, and, having secured his portmanteau, he was before long driving away in the direction of Bloomsbury. His strength was fast ebbing away, and the merciless jolting of the cab evidently tried him to the utmost, but he bore up with the strong endurance of one who knows that at the end of the struggle relief awaits him.

'If he is only at home,' he muttered to himself, 'all will be well. He'll know where I ought to go; he'll do it all for me in the best way. *Ach! Gott in Himmel!* but I need some one!'

With an excruciating jerk the cab drew up before a somewhat grim-looking house; had he arrived at the *Himmel* he had just been speaking of, the traveller could not have given an exclamation of greater relief. He crawled up the steps, over-ruled some question on the part of the servant, and was shown into a brightly-lighted room. At one glance he had taken in the whole of that restful picture so welcome to his sore need. It was a good-sized room, lined with books, which had evidently seen good service, many of them had been bought with the price of foregone meals, almost all of them embodied some act of denial. Above the mantelpiece hung a little oil-painting of a river scene, the sole thing not strictly of a useful order, for the rest of the contents of this study were all admirably adapted for working purposes, but were the reverse of luxurious.

Seated at the writing-table was the master of the house, who had impressed his character plainly enough on his surroundings. He looked up with an expression of blank astonishment on hearing the name of his visitor, then the astonishment changed to incredulity; but, when the weary traveller actually entered the room, he started up with an exclamation of delight which very speedily gave place to dismay when he saw how ill his friend was.

'Why, Haeberlein!' he said, grasping his hand, 'what has happened to you?'

'Nothing very remarkable,' replied Haeberlein, smiling. 'Only a great wish to see you before I die.' Then, seeing that Raeburn's face changed fearfully at these words, 'Yes, it has come to that, my friend, I've a very short time left, and I wanted to see you; can you tell me of rooms near here, and of a decent doctor?'

'Of a doctor, yes,' said Raeburn, 'of one who will save your life, I hope ; and for rooms— there are none that I know of except in this house, where you will of course stay.'

'With the little *Herzblättchen* to nurse me!' said Haeberlein, with a sigh of weary content as he sank back in an arm-chair. 'That would be a very perfect ending, but think what the world would say of you, if I, who have lent a hand to so much that you disapprove, died in your house; inevitably you would be associated with my views and my doings.'

'Maybe!' said Raeburn. 'But I hope I may say that I've never refused to do what was right for fear of unpleasant consequences. No, no, my friend, you must stay here. A hard life has taught me that, for one in my position, it is mere waste of time to consider what people will say ; they will say and believe the worst that can be said and believed about me; and thirty years of this sort of thing has taught me to pay very little regard to appearances.'

As he spoke he took up the end of a speaking-tube which communicated with the green-room, Haeberlein watching his movements with the placid, weary indifference of one who is perfectly convinced that he is in the right hands. Presently the door opened and Erica came in. Haeberlein saw now, what he had half fancied at Salzburg, that, although loving diminutives would always come naturally to the lips when speaking of Erica, she had in truth lost the extreme youthfulness of manner which had always characterised her. It had to a great extent been crushed out of her by the long months of wearing anxiety, and—though she was often as merry and kittenish as ever—her habitual manner was that of a strong, quick temperament kept in check. The restraint showed in everything. She was much more ready to hear and much less ready to speak, her humorous talk was freer from sarcasm, her whole bearing characterised by a sort of quiet steadfastness which made her curiously like her father. His philosophical calm had indeed been gained in a very different way, but in each the calmness was the direct result of exceptionally trying circumstances brought to bear on a noble nature.

'Herr Haeberlein has come here to be nursed,' said Raeburn, when the greetings were over.

'Will you see that a room is got ready, dear?'

He went out into the hall to dismiss the cab, and Haeberlein seized the opportunity to correct his words.

'He thinks I shall get better, but it is impossible, my *Herzblättchen;* it is only a question of weeks now, possibly only of days. Was I wrong to come to you?'

'Of course not,' she said, with the sort of tender deference with which she always spoke to him. 'Did you think father would let you go anywhere else?'

'I didn't think about it,' said Haeberlein, wearily; 'but he wouldn't, you see.'

Raeburn returned while he was speaking, and Erica went away quickly to see to the necessary preparations. Herr Haeberlein had come, and she did not for a moment question the rightness of her father's decision; but yet in her heart she was troubled about it, and she could see that both her aunt and Tom were troubled too. The fact was that for some time they had seen plainly enough that Raeburn's health was failing, and they dreaded any additional anxiety for him. A man cannot be involved in continual and harassing litigation, and at the same time agitate perseveringly for reform, edit a newspaper, write books, rush from Land's End to John o' Groat's, deliver lectures, speak at mass meetings, teach science, befriend every unjustly used person, and get through the enormous amount of correspondence, personal supervision, and inevitable interviewing, which falls to the lot of every popular leader, without sooner or later breaking down.

Haeberlein had come, however, and there was no help for it. They all did their very utmost for him, and those last weeks of tender nursing were perhaps the happiest of his life. Raeburn never allowed anyone to see how the lingering expectation, the dark shadow of the coming sorrow, tried him. He lived his usual busy life, snatching an hour whenever he could to help in the work of nursing, and bringing into the sick-room the strange influence of his strength and serenity.

The time wore slowly on. Haeberlein, though growing perceptibly weaker, still lingered, able now and then to enter into conversation, but for the most part just lying in patient silence, listening with a curious impartiality to whatever they chose to read to him, or whatever they began to talk about. He had all his life been a man of no particular creed, and he retained his curious indifference to the end, though Erica found that he had a sort of vague belief in a First Cause, and a shadowy expectation of a personal existence after death. She found this out through Brian, who had a way of getting at the minds of his patients.

One very hot afternoon she had been with him for several hours, when about five o'clock her father came into the room. Another prosecution under the Blasphemy Laws had just commenced. He had spent the whole day in a stifling law court, and even to the dying man his exhaustion was apparent.

'Things gone badly?' he asked.

'Much as I expected,' said Raeburn, taking up a Marshal Neil rose from the table, and studying it abstractedly. 'I've had a sentence of Auerbach's in my head all day. "The martyrdom of the modern world consists of a long array of thousands of trifling annoyances." These things are in themselves insignificant, but multiplication makes them a great power. You have been feeling this heat, I'm afraid. I will relieve guard, Erica. Is your article ready?'

'Not quite,' she replied, pausing to arrange Haeberlein's pillows while her father raised him.

'Thank you, little *Herzblättchen*,' he said, stroking her cheek, '*auf Wiedersehen.*'

'*Auf Wiedersehen*,' she replied, brightly, and gathering up some papers ran downstairs to finish her work for the *Daily Review*.

A few minutes later, Brian came in for his second visit.

'Any change?' he asked.

'None, I think,' she answered, and went on with her writing with an apprehensive glance every now and then at the clock. The office boy was mercifully late, however, and it must have been quite half an hour after she had left Haeberlein's room that she heard his unwelcome ring. Late as he was, she was obliged to keep him waiting a few minutes, for it was exceedingly difficult in those days to get her work done. Not only was the time hard to obtain, but the writing itself was a difficulty; her mind was occupied with so many other things, and her strength was so overtasked, that it was often an effort almost intolerable to sit down and write on the appointed subject.

She was in the hall giving her manuscript to the boy when she saw her father come downstairs; she followed him into the study, and one look at his face told her what had happened. He was leaning back in the chair in which but a few weeks before she had seen Haeberlein himself; it came over her with a shudder that he looked almost as ill now as his friend had looked. She sat down on the arm of his chair, and slipped her hand into his, but did not dare to break the silence. At last he looked up.

'I think you know it,' he said. 'It is all over, Erica.'

'Was Brian there?' she asked.

'Happily, yes, though there was nothing to be done. The end was strangely sudden and quite painless, just what one would have wished for him. But, oh, child! I can ill spare such a friend just now!'

His voice failed, and great tears gathered in his eyes. He let his head rest for a minute on Erica's shoulder, conscious of a sort of relief in the clasp of arms which had so often, in weak babyhood, clung to him for help, conscious of the only comfort there could be for him as his child's kisses fell on lips, and brow, and hair.

'I am overdone, child,' he said at length, as though to account for breaking down, albeit, by the confession, which but a short time before he would never have made, that his strength was failing.

All through the dreary days that followed, Erica was haunted by those words. The work had to go on just as usual, and it seemed to tell on her father fearfully. The very day after Haeberlein's death it was absolutely necessary for him to speak at a mass meeting in the north of England, and he came back from it almost voiceless, and so ill that they were at their wits' end to know what to do with him. The morrow did not mend matters, for the jury disagreed in the Blasphemy Trial, and the whole thing had to be gone through again.

A more trying combination of events could hardly have been imagined, and Erica, as she stood in the crowded cemetery next day at the funeral, thought infinitely less of the Quixotic Haeberlein—whom she had, nevertheless, loved very sincerely—than of her sorely overtasked father. He was evidently in dread of breaking down, and it was with the greatest difficulty that he got through his oration. To all present the sight was a most painful one, and although the musical voice was hoarse and strained, seeming, indeed, to tear out each sentence by sheer force of will, the orator had never carried his audience more completely with him. Their tears were, however, more for the living than for the dead; for the man who was struggling with all his might to restrain his emotion, painfully spurring on his exhausted powers to fulfil the duty in hand. More than once Erica thought he would have fainted, and she was fully prepared for the small crowd of friends who gathered round her afterwards, begging her to persuade him to rest. The worst of it was that she could see no prospect of rest for him, though she knew how sorely he longed for it. He spoke of it as they drove home.

'I've an almost intolerable longing for quiet,' he said to her. 'Do you remember Mill's passage about the two main constituents of a satisfied life—excitement and tranquillity? How willingly would I change places to-day with that Tyrolese fellow whom we saw last year!'

'Oh! if we could but go to the Tyrol again!' exclaimed Erica; but Raeburn shook his head.

'Out of the question just now, my child; but next week, when this blasphemy trial is over, I must try to get a few days' holiday—that is to say, if I don't find myself in prison.'

She sighed, the sigh of one who is burdened almost beyond endurance. For recent events had proved to her, only too plainly, that her confidence that no jury would be found to convict a man under the old blasphemy laws was quite mistaken.

That evening, however, her thoughts were a little diverted from her father. For the first time for many months she had a letter from Rose. It was to announce her engagement to Captain

Golightly. Rose seemed very happy, but there was an undertone of regret about the letter which was uncomfortably suggestive of her flirtation with Tom. Also there were sentences, which to Erica were enigmatical, about 'having been so foolish last summer,' and wishing that she 'could live that Brighton time over again.' All she could do was to choose the time and place for telling Tom with discrimination. No opportunity presented itself till late in the evening, when she went down as usual to say good night to him, taking Rose's letter with her. Tom was in his 'den,' a small room consecrated to the goddess of disorder—books, papers, electric batteries, crucibles, chemicals, new temperance beverages, and fishing rods were all gathered together in wild confusion. Tom himself was stirring something in a pipkin over the gas-stove when Erica came in.

'An infallible cure for the drunkard's craving after alcohol,' he said, looking up at her with a smile. '"A thing of my own invention," to quote the knight in "Through the Looking-glass." Try some?'

'No, thank you,' said Erica, recoiling a little

from the very odoriforous contents of the pipkin. 'I have had a letter from Rose this evening.'

Tom started visibly.

'What, has Mr. Fane-Smith relented?' he asked.

'Rose had something special to tell me,' said Erica, unfolding the letter.

But Tom just took it from her hands without ceremony, and began to read it. A dark flush came over his face—Erica saw that much, but afterwards would not look at him, feeling that it was hardly fair. Presently he gave her the letter once more.

'Thank you,' he said, in a voice so cold and bitter that she could hardly believe it to be his. 'As you probably see, I have been a fool. I shall know better how to trust a woman in the future.'

'Oh, Tom,' she cried, 'don't let it——'

He interrupted her.

'I don't wish to talk,' he said. 'Least of all to one who has adopted the religion which Miss Fane-Smith has been brought up in—a religion which of necessity debases and degrades its votaries.'

Her eyes filled with tears, but she knew that Christianity would in this case be better vindicated by silence than by words, however eloquent. She just kissed him and wished him good night. But, as she reached the door, his heart smote him.

'I don't say it has debased you,' he said, 'but that that is its natural tendency. You are better than your creed.'

'He meant that by way of consolation,' thought Erica to herself, as she went slowly upstairs fighting with her tears.

But of course the consolation had been merely a sharper stab; for to tell a Christian that he is better than his creed is the one intolerable thing.

What had been the extent of the understanding with Rose Erica never learnt, but she feared that it must have been equivalent to a promise in Tom's eyes, and much more serious than a mere flirtation in Rose's, otherwise the regret in the letter was, from one of Rose's way of thinking, inexplicable. From that time there was a marked change in Tom; Erica was very unhappy about him, but there was little to be done, except, indeed, to share all his interests as much as she could, and to try to make the home-life pleasant. But this was by no means easy. To begin with, Raeburn himself was more difficult than ever to work with, and Tom, who was in a hard, cynical mood, called him overbearing where, in former times, he would merely have called him decided. The very best of men are occasionally irritable when they are nearly worked to death; and, under the severe strain of those days, Raeburn's philosophic calm more than once broke down, and the quick Highland temper, usually kept in admirable restraint, made itself felt.

It was not, however, for two or three days after Haeberlein's funeral that he showed any other symptoms of illness. One evening they were all present at a meeting at the East-end, at which Donovan Farrant was also speaking. Raeburn's voice had somewhat recovered, and he was speaking with great force and fluency, when all at once, in the middle of a sentence, he came to a dead pause. For half a minute he stood perfectly motionless; before him were the densely packed rows of listening faces, but what they had come there to hear he had not the faintest notion. His mind was exactly like a sheet of white paper; all recollection of the subject he had been speaking on was entirely obliterated. Some men would have pleaded illness and escaped, others would have blundered on. But Raeburn, who never lost his presence of mind, just turned to the audience and said, quietly,

'Will some one have the goodness to tell me what I was saying? My memory has played me a trick.'

'Taxation!' shouted the people.

A shorthand writer close to the platform repeated his last sentence, and Raeburn at once took the cue and finished his speech with perfect ease. Everyone felt, however, that it was an uncomfortable incident, and, though to the audience Raeburn chose to make a joke of it, he knew well enough that it boded no good.

'You ought to take a rest,' said Donovan to him, when the meeting was over.

'I own to needing it,' said Raeburn. 'Pogson's last bit of malice will, I hope, be quashed in a few days, and after that rest may be possible.

He is of opinion that "there are mony ways of killing a dog though ye dinna hang him," and, upon my word, he's not far wrong.'

He was besieged here by two or three people who wanted to ask his advice, and Donovan turned to Erica.

'He has been feeling all this talk about Herr Haeberlein; people say the most atrocious things about him, just because he gave him shelter at the last,' she said. 'Really sometimes the accusations are so absurd that we ourselves can't help laughing at them. But though I don't believe in being " done to death by slanderous tongues," there is no doubt that the constant friction of these small annoyances does tell on my father very perceptibly. After all, you know the very worst form of torture is merely the perpetual falling of a drop of water on the victim's head.'

'I suppose since last summer this sort of thing has been on the increase?'

'Indeed it has,' she replied. 'It is worse, I think, than you have any idea of. You read your daily paper and your weekly review, but every malicious, irritating word put forth by every local paper in England, Scotland, or Ireland comes to us, not to speak of all that we get from private sources.'

On their way home they did all in their power to persuade Raeburn to take an immediate holiday, but he only shook his head.

'"Dree out the inch when ye have thol'd the span,"' he said, leaning back wearily in the cab, but taking care to give the conversation an abrupt turn before relapsing into silence.

At supper, as ill-luck would have it, Aunt Jean relieved her fatigue and anxiety by entering upon one of her old remonstrances with Erica. Raeburn was not sitting at the table; he was in an easy-chair at the other side of the room, and possibly she forgot his presence. But he heard every word that passed, and at last started up with angry impatience.

'For goodness sake, Jean, leave the child alone!' he said. 'Is it not enough for me to be troubled with bitterness and dissension outside, without having my home turned into an arguing shop?'

'Erica should have thought of that before she deserted her own party,' said Aunt Jean—

'before, to quote Strauss, she had recourse to "religious crutches." It is she who has introduced the new element into the house.'

Erica's colour rose, but she said nothing. Aunt Jean seemed rather baffled by her silence. Tom watched the little scene with a sort of philosophic interest. Raeburn, conscious of having spoken sharply to his sister, and fearing to lose his temper again, paced the room silently. Finally he went off to his study, leaving them to the unpleasant consciousness that he had been driven out of his own dining-room. But when he had gone the quarrel was forgotten altogether; they forgot differences of creed in a great mutual anxiety. Raeburn's manner had been so unnatural, he had been so unlike himself, that in their trouble about it they entirely passed over the original cause of his anger. Aunt Jean was as much relieved as anyone when before long he opened his door and called for Erica.

'I have lost my address-book,' he said—'have you seen it about?'

She began to search for it, fully aware that he had given her something to do for him just out of loving consideration, and with the hope that it would take the sting from her aunt's hard words. When she brought him the book, he took her face between both his hands, looked at her steadily for a minute, and then kissed her.

'All right, little son Eric,' he said, with a sigh. 'We understand each other.'

But she went upstairs feeling miserable about him, and an hour or two later, when all the house was silent, her feeling of coming trouble grew so much that at length she yielded to one of those strange, blind impulses which come to some people, and crept noiselessly out on to the dark landing. At first all seemed to her perfectly still and perfectly dark; but, looking down the narrow well of the staircase, she could see far below her a streak of light falling across the tiles in the passage. She knew that it must come from beneath the door of the study, and it meant that her father was still at work. He had owned to having a bad headache, and had promised not to be late. It was perplexing. She stole down the next flight of stairs and listened at Tom's door; then, finding that he was still about, knocked softly. Tom, with his feet on the mantelpiece, was solacing himself with a pipe and a novel; he started up, however, as she came in.

'What's the matter?' he asked, 'is anyone ill?'

'I don't know,' said Erica, shivering a little. 'I came to know whether father had much to do to-night; did he tell you?'

'He was going to write to Jackson about a situation for the eldest son of that fellow who died the other day, you know; the widow, poor creature, is nearly worried out of her life, she was here this afternoon. The chieftain promised to see about it at once; he wouldn't let me write, and of course a letter from himself will be more likely to help the boy.'

'But it's after one o'clock,' said Erica, shivering again, 'he can't have been all this time over it.'

'Well, perhaps he is working at something else,' said Tom. 'He's not been sleeping well lately, I know. Last night he got through thirty-three letters, and the night before he wrote a long pamphlet.'

Erica did not look satisfied.

'Lend me your stove for a minute,' she said; 'I shall make him a cup of tea.'

They talked a little about the curious failure of memory noticed for the first time that evening. Tom was more like himself than he had been for several days; he came downstairs with her to carry a light, but she went alone into the study. He had not gone up the first flight of stairs, however, when he heard a cry, then his own name called twice in tones that made him thrill all over with a nameless fear. He rushed down and pushed open the study door. There stood Erica with blanched face; Raeburn sat in his customary place at the writing-table, but his head had fallen forward, and though the face was partly hidden by the desk, they could see that it was rigid and deathly pale.

'He has fainted,' said Tom, not allowing the worse fear to overmaster him. 'Run quick, and get some water, Erica.'

She obeyed mechanically. When she returned, Tom had managed to get Raeburn on to the floor and had loosened his cravat, he had also noticed that only one letter lay upon the desk, abruptly terminating at 'I am, Yours sincerely.' Whether the 'Luke Raeburn' would ever be added, seemed to Tom, at that moment, very doubtful. Leaving Erica with her father, he rushed across the square to summon Brian, returning in a very few minutes with the comforting news that he was at home and would be with them immediately. Erica gave a sigh of relief when the quick, firm steps were heard on the pavement outside; Brian was so closely associated with all the wearing times of illness and anxiety which had come to them in the last six years, that in her trouble she almost forgot the day at Fiesole, regarding him not as her lover, but as the man who had once before saved her father's life. His very presence inspired her with confidence, the quiet authority of his manner, the calm, business-like way in which he directed things. Her anxiety faded away in the perfect consciousness that he knew all about it, and would do everything as it should be done. Before very long Raeburn showed signs of returning consciousness, sighed uneasily—then, opening his eyes, regained his faculties as suddenly as he had lost them.

'Hullo!' he exclaimed, starting up. 'What's all this coil about? What are you doing to me?'

They explained things to him.

'Oh! fainted did I!' he said, musingly. 'I have felt a little faint once or twice lately. What day is it? What time is it?' Tom mentioned the meeting of the previous evening, and Raeburn seemed to recollect himself. He looked at his watch, then at the letter on his desk. 'Well, it's my way to do things thoroughly,' he said, with a smile; ' I must have been off for a couple of hours. I am very sorry to have disturbed your slumbers in this way.'

As he spoke, he sat down composedly at his desk, picked up the pen and signed his name to the letter. They stood and watched him while he folded the sheet and directed the envelope, his writing bore a little more markedly than usual the tokens of strong self-restraint.

'Perhaps you'll just drop that in the pillar on your way home,' he said to Brian. 'I want Jackson to get it by the first post. If you will look in later on, I should be glad to have a talk with you. At present I'm too tired to be overhauled.'

Then, as Brian left the room, he turned to Erica.

'I am sorry to have given you a fright, my child, but don't worry about me, I am only a little overdone.'

Again that fatal admission, which from Raeburn's lips was more alarming than a long catalogue of dangerous symptoms from other men!

There followed a disturbed night, and a long day in a crowded law-court; then one of the most terrible hours they had ever had to endure, while waiting for the verdict, which would either consign Raeburn to prison or leave him to peace and freedom. So horrible was the suspense, that to draw each breath was to Erica a painful effort. Even Raeburn's composure was a little shaken as those eternal minutes dragged on.

The foreman returned. The court seemed to throb with excitement. Raeburn lifted a calm, stern face to hear his fate. He knew, what no one else in the court knew, that this was to him a matter of life and death.

'Are you agreed, gentlemen?'

'Yes.'

People listened breathlessly.

'Do you find the defendant guilty, or not?'

'Not guilty.'

The reaction was so sharp as to be almost overpowering. But poor Erica's joy was but short-lived. She looked at her father's face, and knew that, although one anxiety was ended, another was already begun.

# CHAPTER VIII.

### HALCYON DAYS.

> There is a sweetness in autumnal days,
> Which many a lip doth praise ;
> When the earth, tired a little, and grown mute
> Of song, and having borne its fruit,
> Rests for a little ere the winter come.
> It is not sad to turn the face toward home,
> Even though it show the journey nearly done ;
> It is not sad to mark the westering sun,
> Even though we know the night doth come.
> Silence there is, indeed, for song,
> Twilight for noon,
> But for the steadfast soul and strong
> Life's autumn is as June.
> *From the ' Ode of Life.'*

'ANYTHING in the papers this evening?' asked a young clergyman, who was in one of the carriages of the Metropolitan Railway late in the afternoon of an August day.

'Nothing of much interest,' replied his wife,

handing him the newspaper she had been glancing through. 'I see that wretched Raeburn is ill. I wish he'd die.'

'Oh! broken down at last, has he?' said the other. 'Where is it? Oh yes, I see. Ordered to take immediate and entire rest. Will be paralysed in a week, if he doesn't. Pleasant alternative that! Result of excessive overwork. Fancy calling his blasphemous teaching work! I could hang that man with my own hands!'

Erica had had a long and harassing day. She was returning from the City, where she had gone to obtain leave of absence from Mr. Bircham; for her father was to go into the quietest country place that could be found, and she of course was to accompany him. At the *Daily Review* office she had met with the greatest kindness, and she might have gone home cheered and comforted had it not been her lot to overhear this conversation. Tom was with her. She saw him hastily transcribing the uncharitable remarks, and knew that the incident would figure in next week's *Idol-Breaker*. It was only a traceable instance of the harm done by all such words.

'Will you change carriages?' asked Tom.

'Yes,' she said; and as she rose to go she quietly handed her card to the lady, who, it is to be hoped, learnt a lesson thereby.

But it would be unjust to show only the dark side of the picture. Great sympathy and kindness was shown them at that time by many earnest and orthodox Christians, and though Raeburn used to accept this sympathy with the remark, 'You see, humanity overcomes the baleful influences of religion in the long-run,' yet he was always touched and pleased by the smallest sign of friendliness; while to Erica such considerateness was an inestimable help. The haste and confusion of those days, added to the terrible anxiety, told severely on her strength; but there is this amount of good in a trying bit of 'hurrying life,' the rest, when it comes, is doubly restful.

It was about six o'clock on an August evening when Raeburn and Erica reached the little country town of Firdale. They were to take up their abode for the next six weeks at a village about three miles off, one of the few remaining places in England which maintained its primitive simplicity, its peaceful quiet having never been disturbed by shriek of whistle or snort of engine.

The journey from town had been short and easy, but Raeburn was terribly exhausted by it; he complained of such severe headache that they made up their minds to stay that night at Firdale, and were soon comfortably established in the most charming old inn, which in coaching days had been a place of note. Here they dined, and afterwards Raeburn fell asleep on a big old-fashioned sofa, while Erica sat by the open window, able in spite of her anxiety to take a sort of restful interest in watching the traffic in the street below. Such a quiet, easy-going life these Firdale people seemed to lead. They moved in such a leisurely way; bustle and hurry seemed an unknown thing. And yet this was market-day, as was evident by the countrywomen with their baskets, and by occasional processions of sheep or cattle. One man went slowly by driving a huge pig; he was in sight for quite five minutes, dawdling along, and allowing the pig to have his own sweet will as far as speed was concerned, but occasionally giving him a gentle poke with a stick when he paused to burrow his nose in the mud. Small groups of men stood talking at the corner of the market-place; a big family went by, evidently returning from a country walk; presently the lamps were lighted, and then immense excitement reigned in the little place, for at the corner where the two main streets crossed each other at right angles a cheap-jack had set up his stall, and, with flaring naphtha lamps to show up his goods, was selling by auction the most wonderful clocks at the very lowest prices—in fact, the most superior glass, china, clothing, and furniture that the people of Firdale had ever had the privilege of seeing. Erica listened with no little amusement to his fervid appeals to the people not to lose this golden opportunity, and to the shy responses of the small crowd which had been attracted, and which lingered on, tempted yet cautious, until the cheap-jack had worked himself up into a white heat of energetic oratory, and the selling became brisk and lively.

By-and-by the silvery moonlight began to flood the street, contrasting strangely with the orange glare of the lamps. Erica still leant her head against the window-frame, still looked out dreamily at the Firdale life, while the soft night wind lightly lifted the hair from her forehead, and seemed to lull the pain at her heart.

It was only in accordance with the general peacefulness when by-and-by her father crossed the room, looking more like himself than he had done for some days.

'I am better, Eric,' he said, cheerfully—'better already. It is just the consciousness that there is nothing that need be done. I feel as if I should sleep to-night.' He looked out at the moon-lit street. 'What a perfect night it is!' he exclaimed. 'What do you say, little one, shall we drive over to this rural retreat now? The good folks were told to have everything ready, and they can hardly lock up before ten.'

She was so glad to see him take an interest in anything, and so greatly relieved by his recovery of strength and spirits, that she gladly fell-in with the plan, and before long they set off in one of the wagonettes belonging to the 'Shrub Inn.'

Firdale wound its long street of red-roofed houses along a sheltered valley in between fir-crowned heights; beyond the town lay rich, fertile-looking meadows and a winding river bordered by pollard willows. Looking across these meadows, one could see the massive tower of the church, its white pinnacles standing out sharp and clear in the moonlight. As Raeburn and Erica crossed the bridge leading out of the town, the clock in the tower struck nine, and the old chimes began to play the tune which every three hours fell on the ears of the inhabitants of Firdale.

'" Life let us cherish,"' said Raeburn, with a smile. 'A good omen for us, little one.'

And whether it was the mere fact that he looked so much more cheerful already, or whether the dear old tune, with its resolute good-humour and determination to make the best of things, acted upon Erica's sensitive nature, it would be hard to say, but she somehow shook off all her cares, and enjoyed the novelty of the moonlight drive like a child. Before long they were among the fir-trees, driving along a sandy road, the sweet night air laden with the delicious scent of pine needles, and to the over-worked Londoners in itself the most delicious refreshment. All at once Raeburn ordered the driver to stop, and, getting out, stooped down by the roadside.

'What is it?' asked Erica.

'Heather!' he exclaimed, tearing it up by handfuls and returning to the carriage laden. 'There! shut your eyes and bury your face in that, and you can almost fancy you're on a Scottish mountain. Brian deserves anything for sending us to the land of heather; it makes me feel like a boy again!'

The three miles were all too short to please them; but at last they reached the little village of Millford, and were set down at a compact-looking, white house known as 'Under the Oak.'

'That direction is charming,' said Raeburn, laughing; 'imagine your business letters sent from the *Daily Review* office to "Miss Raeburn, Under the Oak, Millford!" They'll think we're living in a tent. You'll be nicknamed Deborah!'

It was not until the next morning that they fully understood the appropriateness of the direction. The little white house had been built close to the grand old oak which was the pride of Millford. It was indeed a giant of its kind; there was something wonderfully fine about its vigorous spread of branches and its enormous girth. Close by was a peaceful-looking river, flowing between green banks fringed with willow and marestail and pink river-herb. The house itself had a nice little garden, gay with geraniums and gladiolus, and bounded by a hedge of sunflowers which would have gladdened the heart of an æsthete. All was pure, fresh, cleanly, and perfectly quiet. From the windows nothing was to be seen except the village green with its flocks of geese and its tall sign-post; the river describing a sort of horse-shoe curve round it, and spanned by two picturesque bridges. In the distance was a small church and a little cluster of houses, the 'village' being completed by a blacksmith's forge and a post-office. To this latter place they had to pay a speedy visit for, much to Raeburn's amusement, Erica had forgotten to bring any ink.

'To think that a writer in the *Daily Review* should forget such a necessary of life!' he said, smiling. 'One would think you were your little "Cartesian-well" cousin instead of a journalist!'

However, the post-office was capable of supplying almost anything likely to be needed in the depths of the country; you could purchase there bread, cakes, groceries, hob-nailed boots, paper, ink, and most delectable toffee!

The relief of the country quiet was unlike anything which Erica had known before. There was, indeed, at first a good deal of anxiety about her father. His acquiescence in idleness, his perfect readiness to spend whole days without even opening a book, proved the seriousness of his condition. For the first week he was more completely prostrated than she had ever known him to be. He would spend whole days on the river, too tired even to speak, or would drag himself as far as the neighbouring wood and stretch himself at full length under the trees, while she sat by sketching or writing. But Brian was satisfied with his improvement, when he came down on one of his periodical visits, and set Erica's mind at rest about him.

'Your father has such a wonderful constitution,' he said, as they paced to and fro in the little garden. 'I should not be surprised if, in a couple of months, he is as strong as ever; though most men would probably feel such an overstrain to the end of their days.'

After that, the time at Millford was pure happiness. Erica learnt to love every inch of that lovely neighbourhood, from the hill of Rooksbury, with its fir-clad heights, to Trencham Lake nestled down among the surrounding heath hills. In after-years she liked to recall all those peaceful days, days when time had ceased to exist—at any rate, as an element of friction in life. There was no hurrying here, and the recollection of it afterwards was a perpetual happiness. The quiet river where they had one day seen an otter, a marked event in their uneventful days; the farm with its red gables and its crowd of gobbling turkeys; the sweet-smelling fir groves with their sandy paths; and their own particular wood where beeches, oaks, and silvery birch-trees were intermingled, with here and there a tall pine sometimes stately and erect, sometimes blown aslant by the wind.

Here the winding paths were bordered with

golden-brown moss, and sheltered by a tangled growth of bracken and bramble with now and then a little clump of heather or a patch of blue harebells. Every nook of that place grew familiar to them and had its special associations. There was the shady part under the beeches where they spent the hot days, and this was always associated with fragments of 'Macbeth' and 'Julius Cæsar.' There was the cosy nook on the fir hill where in cool September they had read volume after volume of Walter Scott, Raeburn not being allowed to have anything but light literature, and caring too little for 'society' novels to listen to them even now. There was the prettiest part of all down below the bit of sandy cliff riddled with nest holes by the sandmartins; here they discovered a little spring, the natural basin scooped out in the rock, festooned with ivy and thickly coated with the pretty green liverwort. Never surely was water so cold and clear as that which flowed into the basin with its ground of white sand, and overflowed into a little trickling stream; while in the distance was heard the roar of the river as it fell into a small waterfall. There was the ford from which the place was named, and which Erica associated with a long happy day when Brian had come down to see her father. She remembered how they had watched the carts and horses splashing through the clear water, going in muddy on one side and coming out clean on the other. She had just listened in silence to the talk between Brian and her father, which happened to turn on Donovan Farrant.

They discussed the effect of early education and surroundings upon the generality of men, and Raeburn, while prophesying great things for Donovan's future, and hoping that he might live to see his first Budget, rather surprised them both by what he said about his tolerably well-known early life. He was a man who found it very difficult to make allowances for temptations he had never felt, he was convinced that under Donovan's circumstances he should have acted very differently, and he made the common mistake of judging others by himself. His ruggedly honest nature and stern sense of justice could not get over those past failings. However, this opinion about the past did not interfere with his present liking of the man. He liked him much; and when, towards the end of their six weeks' stay at Millford, Donovan invited them to Oakdene, he was really pleased to accept the invitation. He hoped to be well enough to speak at an important political meeting at Ashborough about the middle of October, and as Ashborough was not far from Oakdene, Donovan wrote to propose a visit there *en route.*

At length the last evening came. Raeburn and Erica climbed Rooksbury for the last time, and in the cool of the evening walked slowly home.

'I have always dreaded old age,' he said. 'But I shall dread it no more. This has been a foretaste of the autumn of life, and it has been very peaceful. I don't see why the winter should not be the same, if I have you with me, little one.'

'You'll have me as long as I am alive,' she said, giving his strong hand a little loving squeeze.

'Truth to tell,' said Raeburn, 'I thought a few weeks ago that it would be a case of—

"Here lies Luke Raeburn, who died of litigation!" But, after all, to be able to work to the last is the happiest lot. 'Tis an enviable thing to die in harness.'

They were walking up a hill, a sort of ravine with steep high banks on either side, and stately pines stretching their blue-green foliage up against the evening sky. A red glow of sunset made the dark stems look like fiery pillars, and presently as they reached the brow of the hill the great crimson globe was revealed to them. They both stood in perfect silence watching till it sank below the horizon.

And a great peace filled Erica's heart, though at one time her father's wish would have made her sad and apprehensive. In former times she had set her whole heart on his learning before death that he was teaching error. Now she had learnt to add to 'Thy will be done,' the clause which it takes some of us a lifetime to learn to say, '*Not* my will.'

## CHAPTER IX.

### ASHBOROUGH.

There's a brave fellow! There's a man of pluck!
A man who's not afraid to say his say,
Though a whole town's against him.
LONGFELLOW.

A man's love is the measure of his fitness for good or bad company here or elsewhere.
OLIVER WENDELL HOLMES.

THE week at Oakdene proved in every way a success; Raeburn liked his host heartily, and the whole atmosphere of the house was a revelation to him. The last morning there had been a little clouded, for news had reached them of a terrible colliery accident in the north of England. The calamity had a special gloom about it, for it might very easily have been prevented, the owners having long known that the mine was unsafe.

'I must say it is a little hard to see how such a horrible sin as carelessness of the lives of human beings can ever bring about the greater good which we believe evil to do,' said Erica, as she took her last walk in the wood with Donovan.

''Tis hard to see at the time,' he replied. 'But I am convinced that it is so. The sin is never good, never right; but when men will sin, then the result of the sin, however frightful, brings about more good than the perseverance in sin with no catastrophe would have done. A longer deferred good, of course, than the good which would have resulted by adhering from the first to the right, and so far inferior.'

'Of course,' said Erica, 'I can see that a certain amount of immediate good may result from this disaster. It will make the owners of other mines more careful.'

'And what of the hundred unseen workings that will result from it?' said Donovan, smiling. 'In the first shock of horror one cannot even glimpse the larger view, but later on——'

He paused for a minute; they were down in the valley close to the little church; he opened the gate, and led the way to a bench under the great yew-tree. Sitting here, they could see the recumbent white cross, with its ever fresh crown of white flowers. Erica knew something of the story it told.

'Shall I tell you what turned me from an anti-theist to an atheist?' said Donovan. 'It was the horror of knowing that a little child's life had been ruined by carelessness. I had been taught to believe in a terrific phantom, who was severely just; but when it seemed that the one quality of justice was gone, then I took refuge in the conviction that there could be no God at all. That *was* a refuge for the time, for it is better to believe in no God than to believe in an immoral God, and it was long years before a better refuge found me. Yet, looking back now over these seven and twenty years, I see how that one little child's suffering has influenced countless lives! how it was just the most beautiful thing that could have happened to her!'

Erica did not speak for a moment, she read half-dreamily the words engraved on the tombstone. Nearly sixteen years since that short, uneventful life had passed into the Unseen, and yet little Dot was at this moment influencing the world's history!

She was quite cheerful again as they walked home, and, indeed, her relief about her father's recovery was so great that she could not be unhappy for long about anything. They found Raeburn on the terrace with Ralph and Dolly at his heels, and the two-year-old baby, who went by the name of 'Pickle,' on his shoulder.

'I shall quite miss these bairnies,' he said, as Donovan joined him.

'Gee up, horsey! Gee up!' shouted Pickle, from his lofty perch.

'And oh, daddy, may we go into Gleyshot wiv you?' said Dolly, coaxingly. 'Elica's father's going to give me a play-cat.'

'And me a whip,' interposed Ralph. 'We may come with you, father, mayn't we?'

'Oh! yes,' said Donovan, smiling, 'if Mr. Raeburn doesn't mind a crowded carriage.'

Erica had gone into the house.

'I don't know how to let you go,' said

Gladys. 'We have so much enjoyed having you. I think you had much better stay here till Monday, and leave those two to take care of themselves at Ashborough.'

'Oh, no,' said Erica, smiling, 'that would never do! You don't realise what an event this is to me. It is the first time father has spoken since his illness. Besides, I have not yet quite learnt to think him well enough to look after himself, though of course he is getting quite strong again.'

'Well, since you will go, come and choose a book for your journey,' said Gladys.

'Oh, I should like that,' said Erica, 'a nice, homeish sort of book, please, where the people lived in Arcadia and never heard of lawcourts!'

Early in the afternoon they drove to Greyshot, stopping first of all at the toy-shop. Raeburn, who was in excellent spirits, fully entered into the difficulties of Dolly's choice. At length a huge toy-cat was produced.

'Oh, I should like that one!' said Dolly, clapping her hands, 'what a 'normous, gleat big cat it is!'

'I shouldn't have known what it was meant for,' said Raeburn, scrutinizing the rather shapeless furry quadruped. 'How is it that you can't make them more like cats than this?'

'I don't know, sir, how it is,' said the shopwoman; 'we get very good dogs, and rabbits, and donkeys, but they don't seem to have attained to the making of cats.'

This view of the matter so tickled Raeburn that he left Ralph and Dolly to see the ''normous gleat big cat' wrapped up, and went out of the shop laughing.

But just outside, a haggard, wild-looking man came up to him, and began to address him in excited tones.

'You are that vile atheist, Luke Raeburn!' he cried, 'oh, I know you well enough. I tell you, you have lost my son's soul; do you hear, wretched infidel, you destroyed my son's soul! His guilt is upon you! And I will have vengeance! vengeance!'

'My friend,' said Raeburn, quietly, 'supposing your son had what you call a soul, do you think that I, a man, should be able to destroy it?'

'You have made him what you are yourself,' cried the man, 'an accursed infidel, an incarnate devil! but I tell you I will have vengeance, vengeance!'

'Have the goodness not to come so near my daughter,' said Raeburn; for the man was pushing up roughly against Erica, who had just come out of the shop. The words were spoken in such an authoritative manner that the man shrank back awed, and in another minute the children had rejoined them, and they drove off to the station.

'What was that man saying?' asked Erica.

'Apparently his son has become a Secularist, and he means to revenge himself on me,' said Raeburn. 'If it wouldn't have lost me this train I would have given him in charge for using threatening language. But no doubt the poor fellow was half-witted.'

Donovan had walked on to the station and so had missed this incident, and though for the time it saddened Erica, yet she speedily forgot it in talking to the children. The arrival at Ashborough, too, was exciting, and she was so delighted to see her father once more in the enjoyment of full health and strength that she could not long be disquieted about anything else. It was a great happiness to her to hear him speak upon any subject on which they were agreed, and his reception that evening at the Ashborough Town Hall was certainly a most magnificent one. The ringing cheers made the tears start to her eyes. The people had been roused by his late illness, and though many of them disliked his theological views, they felt that in political matters he was a man whom they could very ill spare. His speech was a remarkably powerful one, and calculated to do great good. Erica's spirits rose to their very highest pitch, and as they went back together to their hotel, she kept both Raeburn and Donovan in fits of laughter. It was long months since her father had seen her so brilliant and witty.

'You are "fey," little one,' he said. 'I prophesy a headache for you to-morrow.'

And the prophecy came true, for Erica awoke the next morning with a sense of miserable oppression. The day, too, was grey and dreary-looking, it seemed like a different world altogether. Raeburn was none the worse for his exertions; he took a quiet day, however, went for a walk with Donovan in the afternoon, and set off in good time for his evening lecture. It was Sunday evening. Erica was going to church with Donovan, and had her walking things on, when her father looked into the room to say good-bye.

'What, going out?' he said. 'You don't look fit for it, Eric.'

'Oh!' she said, 'it is no use to give way to this sort of headache; it's only one's wretched nerves.'

'Well, take care of yourself,' he said, kissing her. 'I believe you are worn out with all these weeks of attendance on a cantankerous old father.'

She laughed and brightened up, going out with him to the head of the stairs, and returning to watch him from the window. Just as he left the door of the hotel, a small child fell face downwards on the pavement upon the opposite

side of the road, and began to cry bitterly.
Raeburn crossed over and picked up the small
elf; they could hear him saying, 'There, there,
more frightened than hurt, I think,' as he brush-
ed the dust from the little thing's clothes.

'How exactly like father!' said Erica, smiling;
'he never would let us think ourselves hurt. I
believe it is thanks to him that Tom has grown
up such a Stoic, and that I'm not a very lachry-
mose sort of being.'

A little later they started for church; but
towards the end of the Psalms Donovan felt a
touch on his arm. He turned to Erica; she
was as white as death, and with a strange,
glassy look in her eyes.

'Come,' she said, in a hoarse whisper, 'come
out with me.'

He thought she felt faint, but she walked
steadily down the aisle. When they were outside, she grasped his arm, and seemed to make
a great effort to speak naturally.

'Forgive me for disturbing you,' she said;
'but I have such a dreadful feeling that something is going to happen. I feel that I must
get to my father.'

Donovan thought that she was probably labouring under a delusion. He knew that she was always very anxious about her father, and that Ashborough, owing to various memories, was exactly the place where this anxiety would be likely to weigh upon her. He thought, too, that Raeburn was very likely right, and that she was rather overdone by the strain of those long weeks of solitary attendance. But he was much too wise to attempt to reason away her fears; he knew that nothing but her father's presence would set her at rest, and they walked as fast as they could to the Town Hall. He was just turning down a street which led into the High Street, when Erica drew him instead in the direction of a narrow by-way.

'Down here,' she said, walking straight on, as though she held some guiding clue in her hand.

He was astonished, as she could not possibly have been in this part of the town before. Moreover, her whole bearing was very strange; she was still pale and trembling, and her ungloved hands felt as cold as ice, while, although he had given her his arm, he felt all the time that she was leading him.

At length a sound of many voices was heard in the distance. Donovan felt a sort of thrill pass through the hand that rested on his arm, and Erica began to walk more quickly than ever. A minute more, and the little by-way led them out into the market-place. It was lighted with the electric light, and to-night the light was concentrated at one end, the end at which stood the Town Hall. Instinctively Donovan's eyes were turned at once towards that brightest point, and also towards the sound, the subdued roar of the multitude which they had heard on their way. There was another sound, too—a man's ringing voice, a stentorian voice which reached them clearly even at that distance. Raeburn stood alone, facing an angry, tumultuous throng, with his back to the closed door of the building, and his tawny eyes scanning the mass of hostile faces below.

'Every Englishman has a right to freedom of speech. You shall not rob me or any other man of a right. I have fought for this all my life, and I will fight as long as I've breath.'

'That shall not be long!' shouted another speaker. 'Forward, brothers! Down with the infidel! Vengeance! vengeance!'

The haggard, wild-looking man who had addressed Raeburn the day before at Greyshot now sprang forward; there was a surging movement in the crowd like wind in a cornfield. Donovan and Erica, hurrying forward, saw Raeburn surrounded on every side, forced away from the door, and at length half-stunned by a heavy blow from the fanatical leader; then, taken thus at a disadvantage, he was pushed backwards. They saw him fall heavily down the stone steps.

With a low cry, Erica rushed towards him, breaking away from Donovan, and forcing a way through that rough crowd as if by magic. Donovan, though so much taller and stronger, was longer in reaching the foot of the steps, and when at length he had pushed his way through the thickest part of the throng, he was hindered; for the haggard-looking man who had been the ringleader in the assault ran into his very arms. He was evidently struck with horror at the result of his mad enterprise, and now meditated flight. But Donovan stopped him.

'You must come with me, my friend,' he exclaimed, seizing the fanatic by the collar.

Nor did he pause till he had handed him over to a policeman. Then once more he forced a passage through the hushed crowd, and at last reached the foot of the steps. He found Erica on the ground, with her father's head raised on her knee. He was perfectly unconscious, but it seemed as if his spirit and energy had been transmitted to his child. Erica was giving orders so clearly and authoritatively that Donovan could only marvel at her strength and composure.

'Stand back!' she was saying, as he approached. 'How can he come-to while you are shutting out the air? Some one go quickly, and fetch a door or a litter. You go, and you.'

She indicated two of the more respectable-looking men, and they at once obeyed her. She looked relieved to see Donovan.

'Won't you go inside, and speak to the people?' she said. 'I have sent for a doctor. If some one doesn't go soon, they will come out, and then there might be a riot. Tell them, if they have any feeling for my father, to separate quietly. Don't let them all out upon these people; there is sure to be fighting if they meet.'

Donovan could not bear to leave her in such a position, but just then a doctor came up, and the police began to drive back the crowd; and, since the people were rather awed by what had happened, they dispersed meekly enough. Donovan went into the Town Hall then, and gradually learnt what had taken place. It seemed that, soon after the beginning of Raeburn's lecture, a large crowd had gathered outside, headed by a man named Drosser, a street preacher, well known in Ashborough and the neighbourhood. This crowd had stormed the doors of the hall, and had created such an uproar that it was impossible to proceed with the lecture. The doors had been quite unequal to the immense pressure from without, and Raeburn, foreseeing that they would give way, and knowing that, if the insurgents met his audience, there would be serious risk to the lives of many, had insisted on trying to dismiss the crowd without, or, at any rate, to secure some sort of order. Several had offered to go with him, but he had begged the audience to keep perfectly still, and had gone out alone— the crowd being so astonished by this unexpected move that they fell back for a moment before him. Apparently his plan would have succeeded very well had it not been for Drosser's deliberate assault. He had gained a hearing from the people, and would probably have dispersed them had he not been borne down by brute force.

It was no easy task to tell the audience what had happened; but Donovan was popular and greatly respected, and, thanks to his tact, their wrath, though very great, was restrained. In fact, Raeburn was so well known to disapprove of any sort of violence that Donovan's appeal to them to preserve order for his sake met with a deep, suppressed murmur of assent. When all was safe, he hurried back to the hotel, where they were glad enough of his services. Raeburn had recovered his senses for a minute, but only to sink almost immediately into another swoon. For many hours this went on: he would partly revive, even speak a few words, and then sink back once more. Every time Erica thought it would end in death, nor could she gather comfort from the looks of either of the doctors or of Donovan.

'This is not the first time I've been knocked down and trampled on,' said Raeburn, faintly, in one of his intervals of consciousness, 'but it will be the last time.'

And though the words were spoken with a touch of his native humour, and might have borne more than one interpretation, yet they answered painfully to the conviction which lay deep down in Erica's heart.

'They let me send a telegram from the *Ashborough Times* office,' said Donovan to her, in one of the momentary pauses. 'I have sent for your cousin and Mrs. Craigie, and for Brian.'

For the first time Erica's outward composure gave way. Her mouth began to quiver and her eyes to fill.

'Oh! thank you,' she said, and there was something in her voice that went to Donovan's heart.

## CHAPTER X.

### MORS JANUA VITÆ.

Therefore to whom turn I but to Thee, the ineffable Name?
   Builder and maker Thou, of houses not made with hands!
What, have fear of change from Thee who art ever the
    same?
   Doubt that Thy power can fill the heart that Thy power
    expands?

And what is our failure here but a triumph's evidence
   For the fulness of the days? Have we withered or
    agonised?
Why else was the pause prolonged but that singing might
    issue thence?
Why rushed the discords in, but that harmony should be
    prized?
                           R. BROWNING.

EARLY on the Monday morning, three anxious-looking travellers arrived by the first train from London, and drove as fast as might be to the Park Hotel at Ashborough. They were evidently expected, for the moment their cab stopped, a door on one of the upper floors was opened, and some one ran quickly down the stairs to meet them.

'Is he better?' asked Aunt Jean.

Erica shook her head, and, indeed, her face told them much more than the brief words of the telegram. She was deathly white, and had that weighed-down look which people wear when they have watched all night beside one who is hovering between life and death. She seemed to recover herself a little as her hand rested for a moment in Brian's.

'He has been asking for you,' she said. 'Do go to him. The faintness has quite passed off, and they say inflammation has set in; he is in frightful pain.'

Her lips grew a shade whiter as she spoke, and, with an effort, she seemed to turn away from some horrible recollection.

'There is some breakfast ready for you in here,' she said to her aunt. 'You must have something before you see him. Oh, I am so glad you have come, auntie!'

Aunt Jean kissed her, and cried a little; trouble always brought these two together, however much they disagreed at other times. Tom did not say a word, but began to cut a loaf to pieces, as though they had the very largest appetites; the great pile of slices lay untouched on the trencher, but the cutting had served its purpose of a relief to his pent-up feelings.

Later on there was a consultation of doctors; their verdict was, perhaps, a little more hopeful than Erica had dared to expect. Her father had received a fearful internal injury, and was in the greatest danger, but there was still a chance that he might recover, it was just possible; and knowing how his constitution had rallied when everyone had thought him dying three years before, she grew very hopeful. Without hope she could hardly have got through those days, for the suffering was terrible. She hardly knew which she dreaded most, the nights of fever and delirium, when groans of anguish came from the writhing lips, or the days with their clear consciousness, when her father never uttered a word of complaint, but just silently endured the torture, replying always, if questioned as to the pain, 'It's bearable.'

His great strength and vigour made it seem all the more piteous that he should now be lying in the very extremity of suffering, unable to bear even the weight of the bed-clothes. But all through that weary time his fortitude never gave way, and the vein of humour which had stood him in such good stead all his life did not fail him even now. On the Monday, when he was suffering torments, they tried the application of leeches. One leech escaped, and they had a great hunt for it, Raeburn astonishing them all by coming out with one of his quaint flashes of wit, and positively making them laugh in spite of their anxiety and sorrow.

The weary days dragged on, the torture grew worse, opium failed to deaden the pain, and sleep, except in the very briefest snatches, was impossible. But at last, on the Thursday morning, a change set in, the suffering became less intense; they knew, however, that it was only because the end was drawing near, and the life energy failing.

For the second time, Sir John Larkom came down from London to see the patient, but everyone knew that there was nothing to be done. Even Erica began to understand that the time left was to be measured only by hours. She learnt it in a few words which Sir John Larkom said to Donovan on the stairs. She was in her own room with the door partly open, eagerly waiting for permission to go back to her father.

'Oh, it's all up with the poor fellow,' she heard the London doctor say. 'A wonderful constitution: most men would not have held out so long.'

At the time the words did not convey any very clear meaning to Erica; she felt no very sharp pang as she repeated the sentence to herself; there was only a curious numb feeling at her heart, and a sort of dull consciousness that she must move, must get away somewhere, do something active. It was at first almost a relief to her when Donovan returned and knocked at her door.

'I am afraid we ought to come to the court,'

he said. 'They will, I am sure, take your evidence as quickly as possible.'

She remembered then that the man Drosser was to be brought up before the magistrates that morning; she and Donovan had to appear as witnesses of the assault. She went into her father's room before she started; he had specially asked to see her. He was quite clear-minded and calm, and began to speak in a voice which, though weak and low, had the old musical ring about it.

'You are going to give evidence, Eric,' he said, holding her hand in his. 'Now, I don't forgive that fellow for having robbed me of life, but one must be just even to one's foes. They will ask you if you ever saw Drosser before; you will have to tell them of that scene at Greyshot, and you must be sure to say that I said, as we drove off, "No doubt the poor fellow is half-witted." Those were my words, do you remember?'

'Yes,' she said, repeating the words after him at his request, 'I remember quite well.'

'Those words may affect Drosser's case very

much, and I don't wish any man to swing for me—I have always disapproved of the death-penalty. Probably, though, it will be brought in as manslaughter—yes, almost certainly. There—go, my child, and come back to me as soon as you can.'

But the examination proved too much for Erica's physical powers; she was greatly exhausted by the terrible strain of the long days and nights of nursing, and when she found herself in a hot and crowded court, pitilessly stared at, confronted by the man who was in fact her father's murderer, and closely questioned by the magistrate about all the details of that Sunday evening, her over-tasked strength gave way suddenly.

She had told clearly and distinctly about the meeting at Greyshot, and had stated positively that in the Ashborough market-place she had seen Drosser give her father a heavy blow, and then push him down the Town Hall steps.

'Can you recollect whether others pushed your father at the same time?' asked the magistrate. 'Don't answer hurriedly; this is an important matter.'

All at once the whole scene came vividly before Erica—the huge crowd, the glare of the lights, her father standing straight and tall, as she should never see him again, his thick white hair stirred by the wind, his whole attitude that of indignant protest; then the haggard face of the fanatic, the surging movement in the black mass of people, and that awful struggle and fall. Was it he who was falling? If so, she was surely with him, falling down, down, endlessly down.

There was a sudden stir and commotion in the court, a murmur of pity, for Luke Raeburn's daughter had fallen back senseless.

When she came to herself, she was lying on the floor of an office-like room, with her head on Mrs. MacNaughton's lap. Brian was bending over her, chafing her hands. A clock in the building struck one, and the sound seemed to recall things to her mind. She started up.

'Oh!' she cried, 'why am I not with my father? Where have you taken me to?'

'It is all right, dear,' said Mrs. MacNaughton, soothingly, 'you shall come back directly you are well enough.'

'I remember it all now,' she said, 'did I finish? Must I go back there?'

It was some relief to know that Donovan had been able to supplement her evidence, and that the examination was in fact over, Drosser having been remanded for a week. She insisted on going back to the hotel at once, and spent the whole of the afternoon and evening with her father. He was not in great pain now but very restless, and growing weaker every hour. He was able, however, to see several of his friends, and though the farewells evidently tried him, he would not refuse to see those who had come hundreds of miles for that last glimpse.

'What does it matter if I am exhausted?' he said, when some one remonstrated with him. 'It will make no difference at all as far as I am concerned, and it will be a happiness to them for the rest of their lives. Besides, I shall not die to-day, perhaps not to-morrow; depend upon it, I shall die hard.'

They persuaded Erica to rest for the first part of the night. She left Tom and Brian to watch, and went to her room, making them promise to call her if there were any signs of change.

At last the full realisation had come to her; though she hated leaving her father, it was yet a sort of relief to get away into the dark, to be able to give way for a moment.

'Anything but this, oh, God,' she sobbed, 'anything but this!'

All else would have been easy enough to bear, but that he should be killed by the violence and bigotry of one who at any rate called himself a Christian, this seemed to her not tolerable. The hope of years had received its deathblow, the life she most loved was sinking away in darkness, the work which she had so bravely taken as her life-work was all but over, and she had failed. Yes, in spite of all her efforts, all her longings, all her love, she had failed, or at any rate apparently failed, and in moments of great agony we do not—

in fact cannot—distinguish between the real and the apparent. Christ Himself could not do it.

She did not dare to let her sobs rise, for it was one of the trials of that time that they were not in their own home, but in a busy hotel where the partitions were thin and every sound could be heard in the adjoining rooms. Moreover, Aunt Jean was sleeping with her, and must not be disturbed. But as she lay on the floor trying to stifle the restrained sobs which shook her from head to foot, trying to check the bitter tears which would come, her thoughts were somehow lifted quite away from the present; strange little memories of her childish days returned to her, days when her father had been to her the living incarnation of all that was noble and good. Often it is not the great events of a child's life which are so vividly remembered; memory seems to be strangely capricious, and will single out some special word or deed, some trifling sign of love, which has stamped itself indelibly upon the brain to bear its golden harvest of responding love through a lifetime. Vividly there came back to her now the eager happiness with which she had awaited a long-promised treat, as a little thing of seven years old. Her father was to take her on some special excursion, she had long ago forgotten what the particular occasion was, only it was something that could come but once, the day lost, the treat would be lost. But the evening before, when she was on the very tip-toe of expectation, a celebrated action for libel had come to an end much sooner than was expected, and when her father returned in the evening he had to tell her that his case was to come on the next day, and that he could not possibly take her. Even now she could recall the bitterness of the disappointment, but not so vividly as the look in her father's face as he lifted her off the floor where she had thrown herself in the abandonment of her grief. He had not said a word then about the enormity of crying, he had just held her closely in his arms, feeling the disappointment a thousand times more than she felt it herself, and fully realising that the loss of such a long-looked-for happiness was to a child what the loss of thousands of pounds would be to a man. He had been patient with her, though she had entirely failed to see why he could not put off the case just for that day!

'You'll understand one day, little one,' he had said, ' and be glad that you have had your share of pain in a day that will advance the cause of liberty.'

She remembered protesting that that was impossible, that she should always be miserable! at which he had only smiled.

Then it came to Erica that the life upon earth was, after all, as compared with the eternal life, what the day is in the life of a child. It seemed everything at the time, but was in truth such a fragment. And as she lay there—in the immeasurably greater agony of later life, once more sobbing, ' I had hoped, I had planned, this is more than I can bear!'—a Comforter infinitely greater, a Father whose love was infinitely stronger, drew her so near that the word 'near' was but a mockery, and told her, as the earthly father had told her with such perfect truth,

'One day you will understand, child, one day you will be glad to have shared the pain!'

In the next room there was for some time quiet. Poor Tom, heavy with grief and weariness, fell asleep beside the fire; Raeburn was for the most part very still, as if wrapped in thought. At length a heavy sigh made Brian ask if he were in pain.

'Pain of mind,' he said, 'not of body. Don't misunderstand me,' he said, after a pause, with the natural fear lest Brian should fancy his secularism failed him at the near approach of death. 'For myself I am content; I have had a very full life, and I have tried always—yes, I think I may say always—to work entirely for the good of Humanity. But I am wretched about Erica. I do not see how the home can be a very happy one for her when I am gone.'

For a moment Brian hesitated; but it seemed to him, when he thought out the matter, that a father so loving as Raeburn would feel no jealousy at the thought that the love he had deemed exclusively his own might, after all, have been given to another.

'I do not know whether I am right to tell you,' he said. 'Would it make you happier to know that I love Erica—that I have loved her for nearly nine years?'

Raeburn gave an ejaculation of astonishment. There was a long silence; for, the idea once suggested to him, he began to see what a likely thing it was, and to wonder that he had not thought of it before.

'I think you are well suited to each other,' he said at last. 'Now I understand your visit to Florence. What took you away again so suddenly?'

Brian told him all about the day at Fiesole. He seemed greatly touched; all the little proofs and coincidences which had never struck him at the time were so perfectly plain now. They were still discussing it when, at about five o'clock, Erica returned. She was pale and sad, but the worn, harassed, miserable look had quite gone. It was a strange time and place for a betrothal.

'Brian has been telling me about the day at Fiesole,' said Raeburn, letting his weak, nerveless hands play about in her hair, as she knelt beside the bed. 'You have been a leal bairn to me, Eric; I don't think I could have spared you then, even though Brian so well deserved you. But now it makes me very happy to leave you to him; it takes away my only care.'

Erica had coloured faintly, but there was an absence of responsiveness in her manner which troubled Raeburn.

'You do still feel as you did at Fiesole?' he asked. 'You are sure of your own mind? You think you will be happy?'

'I love Brian,' she said, in a low voice. 'But, oh, I can't think now about being happy!' She broke off suddenly and hid her face in the bedclothes.

There was silence in the room. In a minute she raised herself, and turned to Brian, who stood beside her.

'You will understand,' she said, looking right into his eyes. 'There is only one thing that I can feel just now. You do understand, I know.'

With a sudden impulse, she threw her arms round his neck and kissed him.

And Brian did understand. He knew, too, that she wanted to have her father to herself. Even in the very fulfilment of his desire, he was obliged to stand aside, obliged even yet to be patient. Never surely had an impulsive, impetuous man a longer training!

When he had gone, Raeburn talked for some time of Erica's future, talked for so long, indeed, that she grew impatient. How trifling now seemed the sacrifice she had made at Fiesole to which he kept on referring!

'Oh, why do you waste the time in talking of me!' she said at last.

'Why!' he said, smiling. 'Because you are my bairn—of what else should I speak or think? For myself, I am very content, dear, though I should have liked a few more years of work. It was not to be, you see; and, in the end, no doubt this will work good to the cause of——' he broke off, unwilling to pain her.

'Ah, child!' he said, after a pause, 'how miserable you and I might have been for these two years if we had not loved each other! You are not to think, little one, that I have not known what your wishes have been for me. You, and Brian, and Osmond, and of late that noble fellow Farrant, have often made me see that Christianity need not necessarily warp the intellect and cripple the life. I believe that for you, and such as you, the system is not rooted in selfishness. But, dear, you are but the exceptions, the rare exceptions! I know that you have wished with all your heart that I should come to think as you do, while I have been wishing you back into the ranks of secularism. Well! it wasn't to be. We each of us lost our wish. But there is this left, that we each know the other to be honest; each deem it a case of honest mistake. I've felt that all along. We've a common love of truth, and a common love of humanity! Oh, little son Eric! spite of all the creeds, we are very near to each other!'

'Very near,' she whispered. And words which Charles Osmond had spoken years ago returned to her memory. 'I think death will be your gate of life! You will wake up, and exclaim, "Who'd have thought it!"'

After all, death would, in a sense, make them

yet nearer! But human nature is weak, and it is hard for us to realise the Unseen! She could not then feel that it was anything but hard, bitter, heart-breaking, that he should be leaving her in this way.

The pain had now almost entirely ceased, and Raeburn, though very restless, was better able to talk than on the previous day. He asked for the first time what was passing in the world, showed special interest in the accounts of the late colliery accident, and was greatly touched by the gallant efforts of the rescuers, who had to some extent been successful. He insisted, too, on hearing what the various papers had to say about his own case, listening sometimes with a quiet smile, sometimes with a gleam of anger in his eyes. After a very abusive article, which he had specially desired to hear, he leant back with an air of weariness.

'I'm rather tired of this sort of thing!' he said, with a sigh. 'What will the *Herald* do when it no longer has me to abuse?'

Of Drosser and of the events of that Sunday

evening he spoke strangely little. What he did say was, for the most part, said to Professor Gosse.

'You say I was rash to go alone,' he replied, when the professor had opened the subject. 'Well, that may be. It is not, perhaps, the first time that in personal matters I've been lacking in due caution. But I thought it would prevent a riot. I still think it did so.'

'And what is your feeling about the whole matter?' asked the professor. 'Do you forgive Drosser for having given you this mortal injury?'

'One must bow to necessity,' said Raeburn, quietly. 'When you speak of forgiving, I don't quite understand you; but I don't intend to hand down a legacy of revenge to my successors. The law will duly punish the man, and future atheists will reap the benefit of my death. There is, after all, you know, a certain satisfaction in feeling that I die as I have lived in defending the right of free speech. I can't say that I could not have wished that Drosser had made an end of me at nine-and-seventy rather than at nine-and-forty. But the people will not forget the manner of my dying. I shall live on in their hearts, and that is a glorious immortality! the only immortality I have ever looked for!"

In the afternoon, to the astonishment of all, Mr. Fane-Smith came over from Greyshot, horrified to hear that the man whom he had once treated with scant justice and actual discourtesy was lying on his death-bed, a victim to religious fanaticism. Spite of his very hard words to her, Erica had always respected Mr. Fane-Smith, and she was glad that he had come at the last. Her aunt had not come; she had hesitated long, but in the end the recollection that Greyshot would be greatly scandalised, and that, too, on the very eve of her daughter's wedding, turned the scale. She sent affectionate messages and a small devotional book, but stayed at home.

Mr. Fane-Smith apologised frankly and fully to Raeburn for his former discourtesy, and then plunged at once into eager questions and eager arguments. He could not endure the thought that the man in whom at the last he was able to recognise a certain nobility of character, should be sinking down into what he considered everlasting darkness. Bitterly did he now regret the indifference of former years, and the actual uncharitableness in which he had of late indulged.

Raeburn lay very passively listening to an impassioned setting forth of the gospel, his hands wandering about restlessly, picking up little bits of the coverlet in that strange way so often noticed in dying people.

'You are mistaken,' he said, when at length Mr. Fane-Smith ceased. 'Had you argued with me in former years, you would never have convinced me, your books and tracts could never have altered my firm convictions. All my life I have had tracts and leaflets showered down upon me, with letters from pious folks desiring my conversion. I have had innumerable letters, telling me that the writers were praying for me. Well, I think they would have done better to pray for some of my orthodox opponents who are leading immoral lives; but, in so far as prayers show a certain amount of human interest, I am very willing that they should pray for me, though they would have shown better taste if they had not informed me of their supplications. But don't mistake me! it is not in this way that you will ever prove the truth of your religion. You must show justice to your opponents, first! You must put a different spirit into your pet word, "Charity." I don't think you *can* do it! I think your religion false! I consider that it is rooted in selfishness and superstition! Being convinced of this when I was still young, I had to find some other system to take its place. That system I found in Secularism. For thirty years I have lived as a Secularist and have been perfectly content, notwithstanding that my life has been a very hard one. As a Secularist I now die content.'

Mr. Fane-Smith shuddered. This was of course inexpressibly painful to him. He could not see that what had disgusted Raeburn with religion had been the distortion of Christ's teaching, and that in truth the Secularist creed embodied much of the truest and loftiest Christianity.

Once more he reiterated his arguments, striving hard to show by words the beauty of his religion. But Christianity can only be vindicated by deeds, can only be truly shown forth in lives. The country, the 'Christian Country,' as it was fond of styling itself, had had thirty years in which to show to Raeburn the loving kindness, the brotherhood, the lofty generosity which each professed follower of Christ ought to show in his life. Now the time was over, and it was too late.

The dying man bent forward, and a hard look came into his eyes, and a sternness overspread his calm face.

'What has Christianity done for me?' he asked. 'Look at my life. See how I have been treated.'

And Mr. Fane-Smith was speechless. Conscience-stricken, he knew that to this there was no reply that *he* could honestly make; and a question dawned upon his mind—Was his own 'Christianity' really that of Christ?

As evening drew on, Raeburn's life was slowly ebbing away. Very slowly, for to the last he fought for breath. All his nearest friends were gathered round him, and to the end he was clearly conscious, and, as in life, calmly philosophical.

'I have been well "friended" all my life,' he said once, looking round at the faces by his bedside.

They were all too broken-hearted to respond, and there were long silences, broken only by the labouring breath and restless movements of the dying man.

Towards midnight there was a low roll of distant thunder, and gradually the storm drew nearer and nearer. Raeburn asked to be raised in bed, that he might watch the lightning, which was unusually beautiful. It was a strange, weird scene—the plainly furnished hotel room, sparsely lighted by candles, the sad group of watchers, the pale, beautiful face of the young girl bending over the pillow, and the strong, rugged Scotchman, with his white hair and keen brown eyes, upon whose face death had already set his pale tokens. From the uncurtained window could be seen the dark outline of the adjacent houses, and the lights lower down the hill scattered here and there throughout the sleeping city. Upon all this the vivid lightning played, and the thunder followed with its mighty crash, rolling and echoing away among the surrounding hills.

'I am glad to have seen one more storm,' said Raeburn.

But soon he grew weary, tired just with the slight exertion of looking and listening. He sighed. To a strong, healthy man in the very prime of life, this failing of the powers was hard to bear. Death was very near; he knew it well enough—knew it by this slow, sure, painless sinking.

He held Erica's hand more closely, and after that lay very still, once or twice asking for more coverings over his feet. The night wore on. After a long silence, he looked up once more and said to Tom,

'I promised Hazeldine a sovereign towards the fund for——' He broke off with a look of intense weariness, adding after an interval—'He'll tell you. See that it's paid.'

The storm had passed, and the golden-red dawn was just breaking, when once more the silence was broken.

'Come nearer, Eric,' he whispered—'nearer!'

Then came a long pause.

There was stillness—that fearful stillness, when the watchers begin to hush their very breath, that they may catch the last faint breathings! Poor Tom could stand it no longer; he just buried his face in his hands and sobbed. Perhaps Erica envied him. Violent grief would surely have been more endurable than this terrible sinking, this dread of not keeping up to the end. Was she falling with him down those horrible steps? was she sinking with him beneath the cold, green waves? Oh, death—cruel death! why had he not taken them together on that summer day?

Yet what was she saying? The death-angel was but God's messenger, and her father could never, never be beyond the care of One who loved him infinitely—eternally! If He the Father were taking him from her, why, she would trust Him, though it should crush her whole world!

'Nearer, Eric—nearer!' How those last words rang in her ears as she waited there with her hands in his. She knew they would be the last, for he was sinking away into a dreamily passive state—just dying because too tired to live.

'Nearer, nearer!' Was this agony indeed to heal the terrible division between them? Ah! mystery of evil, mystery of pain, mystery of death! only the love of the Infinitely Loving can fathom you—only the trust in that Love give us a glimpse of your meaning!

She felt a tightening of the fingers that clasped hers. He was still conscious; he smiled; —just such a smile as he used to give her when, as a little thing, she had fretted about his leaving home.

She pressed her quivering lips to his, clung to him, and kissed him again and again. There was a sigh. A long interval, and another sigh. After that, silence.

## CHAPTER XI.

### RESULTS CLOSELY FOLLOWING.

But that one man should die ignorant who had capacity for knowledge, this I call a tragedy.
CARLYLE.

Not on the clasp of consciousness—on Thee my life depends.

. . . . . . . . . . .

Not what I think, but what Thou art, makes sure.
GEORGE MAC DONALD.

A WAVE of strangely varied feeling swept through the country in the next four-and-twenty hours. From the Raeburnites came a burst of mingled wrath and grief, and a bitter outcry against the religion which inevitably, they thought, tended to produce such fanatics as Drosser. From the poor and oppressed came a murmur of blank despair; they had looked upon Raeburn as the deliverer from so much that now weighed upon them, and were so perfectly conscious that he understood their wants and difficulties in a way which others failed to do, that his death in the very prime of manhood simply stunned them. The liberal-minded felt a thrill of horror and indignation at the thought that such deeds as this could take place in the nineteenth century; realising, however, with a shudder that the rash act of the ignorant fanatic was, in truth, no worse than the murder of hatred, the perpetual calumny and injustice which thousands of professing Christians had meted out to Raeburn. In nothing had the un-Christ-likeness of the age been more conspicuous than in the way in which Raeburn had all his life been treated.

The fashionable world felt a sort of uncomfortableness. The news reached them at their laziest time of year; they came in from shooting-parties to read the account in the papers, they discussed it in ball-rooms and at evening-parties at Brighton and Greyshot, and the other autumnal resorts. 'So he was dead! Well, really they were tired of hearing his name! It was rather horrible, certainly, that his daughter should have seen it all, but such infamous creatures as Raeburn had no business to have daughters. No doubt she would stand it very well—anything, you know, for a little notoriety. Such people lived for notoriety! Of course the papers had put in a lot of twaddle that he had said on his death-bed—"Always had tried to work entirely for the good of humanity," and that sort of nonsense. 'This coffee ice is excellent! Let me get you another;' after which the subject would be dropped, and the speakers would return to the ball-room to improve upon Raeburn's life, which they presumed so severely to criticise, by a *trois temps* enlivened by a broad flirtation.

Here and there a gleam of good was effected, inasmuch as some of the excessively narrow began to see what narrowness leads to. Mr. Cuthbert, coming home from his annual Swiss tour, was leaning back sleepily in a first-class carriage at the Folkestone station, when the voice of a newsboy recalled him to the everyday world with a slight shock. There was the usual list of papers; he was sleepy and thought he would not get one, but then came the loud voice, not a couple of yards from his ear, 'Death of Mr. Raeburn! Death of Luke Raeburn this da-ay!'

Mr. Cuthbert had his head out of the window in a moment.

'Here, paper!'

'These boys will call anything to sell their papers,' he remarked to his companion; 'I daresay it's nothing more than a rumour.'

'Precious good thing for the country if it was true,' replied the other, a young fellow of two-and-twenty who dawdled through life upon an income of £5,000 a year, and found it quite possible to combine the enjoyment of lax living with the due expression of very orthodox sentiments.

Mr. Cuthbert did not answer; his eye was travelling down a column of the newspaper, and he felt a curious pricking of remorse as he read. He had once been rude to Erica Raeburn;

he had all his life retailed dubious stories about her father, knowing all the time that had anyone believed such stories of himself upon such shaky evidence, he would have used very strong language about them. And now this fellow was dead! Curiously enough, Mr. Cuthbert, who had many times remarked that 'Raeburn ought to be shut up, or better still hung,' was now the one to wish him alive again. Ugh! it was a horrible story. He quite shivered as he read the account of those days of torture.

But in a room at the Park Hotel, Ashborough, two very different men were discussing the same subject. Mr. Fane-Smith, with all his faults, had always been well-intentioned, and though frightful harm may be done by people with good intentions, they can never stand upon the same level as those who wilfully and maliciously offend. All too plainly now he saw how grievously he had failed with regard to Raeburn, and patiently did he listen to Donovan's account of the really good work which Raeburn had effected in many instances.

'Much as you may hate his views, you must

at least see that, as some one has well expressed it, " It takes a high-souled man to move the masses even to a cleaner stye." And I say that a man who worked as he worked, striving hard to teach the people to live for the general good, advocating temperance, promoting the spread of education, and somehow winning those whom no one else had ever touched to take an intelligent interest in politics, in science, and in the future of the race, that such a man claims our respect however much we may disagree with him.'

'But that he should have died ignorant like this!' exclaimed Mr. Fane-Smith, with a shudder.

' 'Tis in truth a tragedy,' said Donovan, sighing. 'But I can well believe that in another world the barriers which he allowed to distort his vision will be removed; the very continuance of existence would surely be sufficient.'

'You are a universalist,' said Mr. Fane-Smith, not in the condemnatory tone he would once have assumed, but humbly, anxiously, like one who gropes his way in a dark place.

'Yes,' replied Donovan. 'Believing in a universal Father, I am naturally that. Upon any other system, what do you make of the good which exists in so many of those who deny all in which you believe? Where does the good go to? I stood beside the death-bed of that noble man this morning. At the very last I saw most touching proofs of his strong sense of justice, his honesty, his desire to promote the good of others, his devotion to his child. Can you believe that all that goodness, which of necessity comes from God, is to go down into what you call everlasting punishment? Don't mistake me. Thank God there is a punishment which no one would wish to forego, such punishment, such drawing forth of the native good, such careful help in the rooting out of what is evil as all good fathers give to their children.'

They were interrupted by the opening of the door. Mr. Fane-Smith started and almost trembled when, on turning round, he saw Erica. She was pale, but preternaturally calm—looking, however, they all felt, as if in her father's death she had received her own death-blow.

'I thought I heard you,' she said, in that

strangely 'gravened' voice which is sometimes one of the consequences of great and sudden trouble. 'Has Donovan taken you into the next room? Will you come?'

For his life Mr. Fane-Smith could not have refused anything which she asked him; there was something in her manner that made the tears rush to his eyes, though he was not, as a rule, easily moved.

He followed her obediently, though with a sort of reluctance; but when he was once there he was glad. Ever since the previous day he had not been able to rid himself of that stern, hard look with which Raeburn had so terribly rebuked him; it had persistently haunted him. There was nothing stern in this dead face. It was still and passionless, bearing the look of repose which, spite of a harassed life, it had always borne in moments of leisure. He hardly looked as though he were dead. Erica could almost have fancied that he was but resting after the toils of a hard day, having fallen asleep for a few minutes as she had often seen him in his arm-chair on a Sunday evening.

Mr. Fane-Smith did not say a word, his eyes wandered from the calm face to the still hands which clasped some sprigs of his native heather, the heather which Donovan's children had sent only the day before, but just in time to win one of his last smiles. Donovan and Erica spoke together in low tones, but something in the sound of that 'gravened' voice arrested Mr. Fane-Smith's attention. He had not heard what had passed before, and there was nothing special in the words that fell now upon his ear, it was rather that his own soul was in a state of receptivity, and so through the first channel that came to hand he was able to receive a new truth.

'I am only his child; God is his Father.'

And there, by the lifeless body of Luke Raeburn, one, who during his life had judged him with the very hardest judgment, learnt for the first time what Fatherhood means.

As long as there was anything to be done, Erica struggled on, although the days were terribly hard, and were rendered infinitely harder by the sort of publicity which attended them. There was the necessity of appearing at the inquest—there was the necessity of reading every word that was written about her father. She could not help reading the papers, could not keep her hands off them, though even now most cruel things were said. There was the necessity of attending the great public funeral in London, of seeing the thousands of grief-stricken people, of listening to the professor's words so broken with sobs that they could hardly be heard. A week later there was the necessity of going down to the Ashborough assizes to appear as a witness in the trial of Drosser.

'What do you feel towards this man?' some one asked her once.

'A great pity,' she replied. 'It is not nearly so hard for me to forgive this poor fanatic, as to forgive those who have taught him his dark creed, or to forgive those who, while calling themselves Christians, have hated my father with the hatred that is quite as bad as murder.'

But when the trial was over, and there was

no longer any necessity to do anything, Erica suddenly broke down. She had never till now yielded, though not a night had passed in which she had not been haunted by the frightful recollections of that Sunday evening and the days following. But the evening she returned from Ashborough she could hold out no longer.

Very quietly she bore that sad return to the empty house, going into all the familiar rooms and showing no sign of grief, because those she loved were with her, watching her with the anxious solicitude which people cannot help showing at such a time, though it is usually more of a trial than a comfort. Erica longed inexpressibly to be alone, and when at length, deceived by her unnatural calm, they were persuaded to leave her, she crept down to the study and shut herself in, and no longer tried to resist the inevitable. The mere surroundings were quite sufficient to open the flood-gates of her grief: the books which her father had loved, the table, the empty chair, the curious cactus which they had brought back from Italy, and in the growth of which they had taken such an interest! the desk at which her father had toiled for so many long years. She hid her face from the light, and broke into a passionate fit of weeping. Then exhausted, nerveless, powerless, she could no longer cope with that anguish of remembrance which was her nightly torment. Once more there rose before her that horrible scene in the Ashborough market-place; once more she could see the glare of light, the huge crowd, the sudden treacherous movement, the fall; once more she heard the crash, the hushed murmur; once more felt the wild struggle to get through that pushing jostling, throng that she might somehow reach him. That nightmare recollection only gave place to a yet more painful one, to the memory of days of such agony that to recall them was almost to risk her reason. She had struggled bravely not to dwell upon these things, but this night her strength was gone, she could do nothing, and Brian, coming at last to seek her, found that the climax he had long foreseen had come.

'Oh,' she sobbed, 'if you love me, Brian, be

willing to let me go! Don't pray for me to live! promise that you will not!'

A shade came over Brian's face. Was the dead father still to absorb all her love? Must he even now resign all to him? Lose Erica at last after these long years of waiting! There was a look of agony in his eyes, but he answered quietly and firmly,

'I will pray only that God's will may be done, darling.'

A sort of relief was apparent in Erica's flushed, tear-stained face, as though he had given her leave to be ill.

After that, for long, weary weeks she lay at the very gate of death, and those who watched by her had not the heart to wish her back to life again.

## CHAPTER XII.

### A NEW YEAR'S DAWN.

And the murky planets, I perceived, were but cradles for the infant spirits of the universe of light . . . And in sight of this immeasurability of life no sadness could endure . . . And I exclaimed, Oh! how beautiful is death, seeing that we die in a world of life and of creation without end! And I blessed God for my life upon earth, but much more for the life in those unseen depths of the universe which are emptied of all but the Supreme Reality, and where no earthly life or perishable hope can enter.

RICHTER.

For many weeks Erica had scarcely a conscious interval. Now and then she had been dimly aware that Brian was in the room, or that Aunt Jean, and Mrs. MacNaughton, and her many secularist friends were nursing her; but all had been vague, dream-like, seen through the distorting fever-mist. One night, however, she woke after a sleep of many hours to see things once more as they really were. There was her little room, with its green-panelled walls, and its familiar pictures, and familiar books. There was Aunt Jean sitting beside the fire, turning over the pages of an *Idol-Breaker,* while all the air seemed to be ringing and echoing with the sound of church bells.

'Auntie,' she said, 'what day is it?'

Aunt Jean came at once to the bed-side.

'It is New-Year's-Day,' she said; 'it struck twelve about five minutes ago, dear.'

Erica made no comment, though the words brought back to her the sense of her desolation —brought back to her, too, the remembrance of another New Year's Day long ago, when she had stood beside her father on the deck of the steamer, and the bells of Calais had gaily pealed in spite of her grief. She took the food her aunt brought her, and promised to go to sleep once more.

'I shall have to wake up again to this misery!' she thought to herself. 'Oh, if one could only sleep right on!'

But God sometimes saves us from what we have most dreaded; and when, at sunrise, Erica woke once more, before any recollection returned to her mind, she became conscious of One who said to her, ' Lo, I am with you alway! Behold I make all things new!'

Streaks of golden light were stealing in between the window-curtains. She lay quite still, able to face life once more in the strength of that Inner Presence; able to endure the well-known sights and sounds, because she could once more realise that there was One Who made even 'the wrath of man to praise' Him; Who, out of blackest evil and cruellest pain, could at length bring good. Presently, passing from the restfulness of that conscious communion, she remembered a strange dream she had had that night.

She had dreamed that she was sitting with Donovan in the little churchyard at Oakdene; in her hand she held a Greek testament, but upon the page had only been able to see one sentence. It ran thus, ' Until the times of the Restitution of all things.' Donovan had insisted that the word should rightly be 'restoration.' She had clung to the old rendering. While they discussed the distinction between the words, a beautiful girl had all at once stood before them. Erica knew in an instant who it must be by the light which shone in her companion's face.

'You are quite right,' she had said, turning her beautiful eyes upon him. 'It is not the mere giving back of things that were, it is the perfecting of that which was here only in ideal; —it is the carrying out of what might have been. All the time there has been progress, all the time growth, and so restoration is better, wider, grander than anything we could dream of here!'

And, as she left them, there had come to both a sort of vision of the Infinite, in sight of which the whole of earthly existence was but as an hour, and the sum of human suffering but as the pin-prick to a strong man, and yet both human suffering and human existence were infinitely worth while. And over them stole a wonderful peace as they realised the greatness of God's universe, and that in it was no wasted thing, no wasted pain, but order where there seemed confusion, and a soul of goodness where there seemed evil.

And, after all, what was this dream compared with the reality which she knew to exist? Well, it was perhaps a little fragment, a dim shadow, a seeing through the glass darkly; but mostly it was a comfort, because she was all the time conscious that there was an infinitely Better which it has not entered into the heart of man to conceive.

Brian came in for his morning visit with a face so worn and anxious that it made her smile.

'Oh!' she said, looking up at him with quiet, shining eyes, 'how I have been troubling you all these weeks! But you are not to be troubled any more, darling. I am going to get better.'

And with a sort of grateful, loving tenderness, she drew his face down to hers and kissed him.

'Where is Tom?' she asked presently, beginning for the first time to take interest in the world again.

'Tom has gone to Oakdene for a day or two,' said Brian. 'He is going to be Donovan's private secretary.'

'How glad I am!' she said. 'Dear old Tom, he does so deserve to be happy!'

'They want you to go there as soon as you are well enough to be moved,' said Brian.

'I should like that,' she said, with a touch of her old eagerness of manner. 'I want to get well quickly; there is so much work for us to do, you know. Oh, Brian! I feel that there is work which *he* would wish me to do, and I'm so glad, so glad to be left to do it!'

Brian thought of the enormous impetus given to the cause of secularism by Raeburn's martyrdom. The momentary triumph of bigotry and intolerance had, as in all other ages, been followed by this inevitable consequence—a dead loss to the persecuting side. Would people at length learn the lesson? Would the reign of justice at length dawn? Would the majority at length believe that the All-Father needs not to be supported by persecuting laws and unjust restrictions?

Yet it was not these thoughts which brought the tears to his eyes—it was the rapture caused by Erica's words.

'My darling will live, and is glad to live!' he thought. 'Who could bear witness to the truth so well! Who be so sweet a reconciler!'

'Why, Brian!—Brian!' exclaimed Erica, as the great drops fell on her hand lying clasped in his.

And there was that in tone and look and touch which made Brian more than content.

THE END.

LONDON: PRINTED BY DUNCAN MACDONALD BLENHEIM HOUSE.

www.ingramcontent.com/pod-product-compliance
Lightning Source LLC
Chambersburg PA
CBHW032044230426

43672CB00009B/1467